Released from
Samford University Library

PRAISE FOR *THE LAWYER MYTH:*

"This book was a long time coming and is a must read for all who want to understand the legal profession. The authors show us the essential role lawyers have in preserving our rights and freedom. This book demonstrates that lawyers are guardians of the rule of law."

—*William G. Paul, Past President, American Bar Association*

"As deans of American law schools for over thirty years, Rennard Strickland and Frank Read have sent generations of bright, dedicated, public-spirited young students into a profession too often maligned as parasitic and unhealthy. *The Lawyer Myth* is their cri de coeur on behalf of the legal profession. In sprightly and jargon-free prose, the authors explain the role of lawyers in maintaining American freedoms and the rule of law. This book should be required reading for critics of the legal profession— and for every young person thinking of studying law."

—*John C. Jeffries Jr., Dean, Emerson Spies Professor of Law, and Arnold H. Leon Professor of Law, University of Virginia School of Law*

"Legitimately concerned about public misperceptions of the legal profession while also being deeply committed to equal justice, Deans Strickland and Read have produced an important and passionately written critique of the importance of the rule of law and the critical, affirmative role of lawyers. What the authors do not discuss, out of modesty, is their iconic stature in legal education and the broader legal community. Their message is beautifully crafted, and the messengers deserve our attention and respect."

—*Hulett H. Askew, ABA Consultant on Legal Education*

"Two longtime law professors and former law school deans are 'mad as hell' about the destructive myths and misconceptions about lawyers and the legal system perpetuated by uninformed and unfair media treatment, political comment, and public misunderstanding. They have assembled, in highly readable form, the empirical data, the historical perspective, and an excellent description of legal training and practice that should set the stage for a more thoughtful and rational discussion of what Americans really believe about the rule of law. This book intends to engage idealistic young people considering careers having to do with law, but it will equally engage every lawyer, judge, public servant, and American citizen who cares about our constitutional system of government and the concept of justice under law on which it is predicated."

—*Christine M. Durham, Chief Justice, Utah Supreme Court*

"In the turmoil of our contemporary society, this book is a much needed manifesto proclaiming the importance of lawyers and judges in maintaining the rule of law in the lives of all citizens."

—*James P. White, ABA Consultant on Legal Education Emeritus*

THE LAWYER MYTH

Rennard Strickland and Frank T. Read

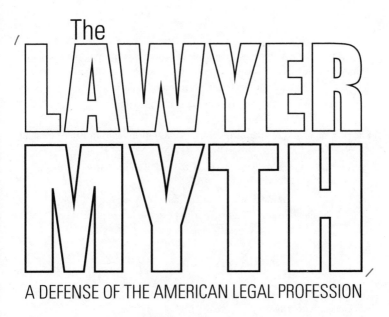

The
LAWYER
MYTH

A DEFENSE OF THE AMERICAN LEGAL PROFESSION

SWALLOW PRESS / OHIO UNIVERSITY PRESS
ATHENS

Samford University Library

Swallow Press / Ohio University Press, Athens, Ohio 45701
www.ohioswallow.com

© 2008 by Ohio University Press

All rights reserved

To obtain permission to quote, reprint, or otherwise reproduce or distribute
material from Ohio University Press / Swallow Press publications, please
contact our rights and permissions department at
(740) 593-1154 or (740) 593-4536 (fax).

The parable of the Keeper of the Springs was reprinted from Peter Marshall,
Mr. Jones, Meet the Master: Sermons and Prayers (New York: F. H. Revell, 1949), by
permission of Revell, a division of Baker Publishing Group, © 1949

Printed in the United States of America
Swallow Press / Ohio University Press books are printed on
acid-free paper ⊗ ™

16 15 14 13 12 11 10 09 08   5 4 3 2 1

Library of Congress Cataloging-in-Publication Data
Strickland, Rennard.
 The lawyer myth : a defense of the American legal profession / Rennard
Strickland and Frank T. Read.
    p. cm.
 Includes bibliographical references.
 ISBN-13: 978-0-8040-1110-5 (cloth : alk. paper)
 ISBN-10: 0-8040-1110-9 (cloth : alk. paper)
 ISBN-13: 978-0-8040-1111-2 (pbk. : alk. paper)
 ISBN-10: 0-8040-1111-7 (pbk. : alk. paper)
 1. Lawyers—United States. 2. Practice of law—United States. I. Read,
Frank T., 1938– II. Title.

KF298.S775 2008
340.023'73—dc22

2007048393

KF
298
.S775
2008

For our bright and dedicated law students,
past and present,
and especially the coming generations
of America's lawyers

In viewing the Americans and studying their laws we perceive that the authority they have entrusted to members of the legal profession, and the influence these individuals exercise in government, are the most powerful existing security against the excesses of democracy.

—Alexis de Tocqueville, *Democracy in America*

CONTENTS

PREFACE

The purpose of this book is to explain and celebrate the rule of law and the role of the legal profession in American life. It explores the significance of America's lawyers in this time of social, economic, and political change. It addresses the position of lawyers as a balancing force in America. Never has there been a greater need for a clear understanding of the lawyer in a democratic society. This work is intended for three broad audiences: (1) The next generation of lawyers, prospective law school students seeking a career and life calling; (2) average citizens, the general public, who need to know more fully how law and lawyers work; and (3) present lawyers and judges charged with operating, improving, and reforming law and lawyering.

Lawyers and judges loom large in twenty-first-century America, and it is crucial to the survival of our social and political institutions that the public understand the centrality of these callings to the preservation of liberty and the rule of law. It is equally important that practicing lawyers and judges be inspired to strengthen these principles for future generations and that the legal profession attract bright young women and men to continue the traditions established by their predecessors.

This book is our tribute to the legal profession and to those individuals who use the law to preserve and protect the best in our society. It uses simple language—nonlegalese—to explain the operation of the law and to expose popular myths and often erroneous charges against lawyers, judges, and the legal system. Our hope is that young women and men who are seriously considering law as their profession will better understand how they, as lawyers, can help create a more just society. We also suggest reforms that will advance the rule of law.

Let there be no mistake about it: this is a highly personal statement affirming the rule of law and defending the role of lawyers. It was inspired by growing attacks on the legal profession, the judiciary, trial by jury, and the rule of law itself. It is written from the perspective of two lifelong legal educators. Like the protagonist in the film *Network* (1976), we are mad as hell, and this tribute and defense is our declaration that we're not going to take it any longer. With more than three-quarters of a century of teaching and deaning between us, we have watched thousands of America's brightest, most spiritually centered, profoundly competent, deeply determined, and dedicated young women and men pass through law school to join the ranks of attorneys, counselors at law, and judges. We believe in them and in their enterprise. We have witnessed what they and their colleagues have done to improve and protect American life, and, while acknowledging that no profession is perfect, we applaud their service.

At the beginning of the twenty-first century, law is fast becoming America's number-one spectator sport. The struggle for justice has become a prime-time event. Court TV is a full-time network; a dozen self-styled judges decide disputes on television; *Law and Order* is television's longest-running dramatic series. Documentaries, TV movies of the week, news hours, and entertainment specials focus on real and imagined disputes, both criminal and civil.

But the prominence of law and the legal profession in American society has led to an abundance of overheated rhetoric. For an illustration of this sort of hyperbole about the law and lawyers, one need only look at the comments of televangelist (and lawyer) Pat Robertson. In 2005, he proclaimed that opposition to the confirmation of certain of his favorite lawyers as federal judges was a crime worse than those committed by al Qaeda. Today, many state and federal legislators propose draconian restrictions on the historic rule of law, even suggesting limits on basic legal rights, such as the use of the jury in civil cases.

Much of this hysteria is fueled by myths and urban legends about preposterous legal cases, many of which have no roots in reality. These include elaborately embellished retellings of runaway lawsuits—the octogenarian burned by spilled McDonald's coffee, the psychic awarded millions for the loss of clairvoyant powers, the phantom Winnebago left on cruise control, the amateur gardener who used his lawn mower as a hedge clipper, or the obese fast-food junkies made rich by suing Burger King. Furthermore, Americans are mesmerized by the criminal cases of such celebrities as Michael Jackson and Martha Stewart or by the civil saga of the burial of Anna Nicole Smith. Nonentities like Scott Peterson become public figures as a result of being charged in criminal court or engaging in civil action. That there is no media shame in exploitation of the law is shown by the publication of O. J. Simpson's hypothetical confession in a tell-all book. Indeed, there was even a short-lived television series called simply *CJ: Celebrity Justice*.

In light of this law-as-sport mentality, the line between legal fact and fiction, legend and reality, becomes difficult to draw. Our courts remain the most open and transparent of the branches of the American democracy. Trial courts and their officers—the lawyers and judges—work with bright lights, if not television cameras, shining directly in their faces. They are under extraordinary pressures, subject to angry denunciations and preposterous charges. The open and public nature of the judicial process allows us to see directly into the operation of the legal system and thus to scrutinize the roles of lawyers and judges in our democracy. We believe that if our system of justice is to survive, prospective lawyers and the American public must know more about law and lawyering than can be learned from a daily dose of Judge Judy or the ritual skewering of the hapless judge-of-the-day by Bill O'Reilly.

Even at the highest level of national discourse, American society has lost touch with the need for the lawyer's skill and has begun to blame unrelated societal dysfunctions on the legal profession. A typical example is President George W. Bush's effort in the 2004 presidential debates to blame the shortage of flu vaccine manufactured in a British pharmaceutical facility on fear of lawsuits by American lawyers.

Ironically, Bush's own recourse to professional legal assistance during the disputed presidential election in 2000 illustrates the point that those who yell loudest in attacking lawyers run quickest to court. Bill O'Reilly and Rush Limbaugh, both outspoken critics of the rule of law, also went on the offensive with trusted attorneys by their sides when they were confronted with allegations that threatened their reputations, careers, and economic interests—not to mention tort reformer Robert Bork's audacity in seeking punitive damages in his slip-and-fall accident at the Yale Club in Manhattan. Surely O'Reilly and Limbaugh and Bork would affirm that at these devastating personal moments, their lawyer was an indispensable professional.

We were inspired to write this book by decades of observing the hypocrisy of media critics of lawyers and the judiciary—from both right and left. Careful observers of the rhetoric of these critics will note that their style is to make loud assertions and bold headlines with precious little factual support. Furthermore, even when the facts become available, these demagogues merely repeat the original premise at an even louder volume. Retractions or corrections never seem to catch up with the initial story.

Thoughtful students of modern America may well ask, "If lawyers are so crucial to our democratic life, what motivates these constant attacks on the legal profession?" At the heart of our book is an analysis of the natural tension between those who see the law as a regulator and upholder of societies' perceived and traditional values and those who see the law as a tool to challenge and change those values.

In the process of writing this book, we have gone from mad as hell about the slander of lawyers and judges to prouder than proud of the legal profession and of what our colleagues are doing to protect Americans and their constitutional rights. We have also come to understand that these attacks on lawyers and judges are attacks on the rule of law, the right to trial by jury, and the ability of society to adapt peacefully to changing social, political, and economic conditions. More is at stake than the feelings of those who have been unfairly bashed by antilawyer critics. As one lay observer noted, "When I was in school, what critics now dismiss as legal technicalities we called constitutional rights."

We deeply resent the fact that many of the faults of modern society are blamed on lawyers, when the legal profession, in fact, systematically struggles to bring balance and reform in a complex and changing world. Public discourse on major issues should not be a game of kick-the-can, with lawyers as the can for kicking. For too long, we as legal educators have said nothing. We have let jokesters and critics take potshots at our professional colleagues, while disgruntled litigants selfishly complain about their own cases and politically motivated ideologues attack judges. We are speaking out now because national leaders and public commentators are making more and more absurd charges, calling the law an instrument of tyranny or declaring that lawsuits are evil. Enough is enough! It is time for us to speak out in defense of the rule of law and the practicing bar and the sitting judiciary. It is time to explain why lawyers are democracy's indispensable servants and how the institutions of the law safeguard our ability to address changing economic, social, and political issues. The American people need to understand that regardless of our political persuasion, in the final analysis, law and lawyers protect all of us. It is not accidental that the balanced scale is a symbol of justice.

Lawyers and judges have become scapegoats for the problems of our age. If crime is up, blame the lawyers and judges. If there is a shortage of flu vaccine, blame the lawyers and judges. If medical costs are skyrocketing, blame the lawyers and judges. If divorce and domestic violence are epidemic, blame the lawyers and judges. If obesity is a national plague, blame the lawyers and judges. If medical malpractice insurance is costly, blame the lawyers and judges. The lawyer blame game is an almost unending litany of the woes of modern society. Among the most absurd of the sins for which lawyers and judges are being asked to atone are overweight children, the collapse of bickering Little Leagues, and a drop in milk production under daylight saving time.

On one hot July day, Donald Trump proclaimed that prenuptial agreements were necessary only because of "sleazy lawyers"; that same day, President George W. Bush asserted that the nation could not have "both lawyers and small business." Even more absurd is the assertion of a group of Olympic divers that losses in their sport in the games in Athens could be traced back to the threat of lawsuits brought against swimming pool operators with allegedly dangerous diving boards.

Modern life is indeed complex and often dark and disturbing, but lawyers and judges are neither the creators nor the perpetuators of this state of affairs. To state the obvious: Lawyers don't sue people—people sue people. And corporations sue corporations. As a nation, we have come to take lawyers and their contributions to society for granted. We should ask where our society would be without lawyers and to whom we would turn if the legal profession did not exist.

Our book is a brief primer on law and lawyers in American society. In the initial chapter, we provide the information necessary to create an understanding and a broad overview of the legal profession and the rule of law, setting forth hard data on the nature, the numbers, and the economics of the legal profession in both a historic and a comparative setting. But we believe that statistics alone do not tell the whole tale, so we turn to cases that illustrate the operation of the law in the lives of individual citizens. We invite readers into the first year of law school through our orientation speeches designed to socialize and welcome prospective lawyers into the profession. Thus, we set forth what we believe to be the function and values brought to our society by America's lawyers.

We then turn in chapter 2 to some common myths and misunderstandings about American law and lawyers. We examine, in considerable detail, differences between facts and popular myths. We focus specifically on two great myths: the charges that there are too many lawyers and too many lawsuits. By comparing America to other industrialized societies, we provide the statistics to refute these misconceptions and, in the process, seek to impart a better understanding of the role of the lawyer in a rapidly changing society. We directly confront cases that are alleged to support the mythology, including the oft-reported McDonald's hot coffee case. We break down the accusations that lawyers and lawsuits have created a medical malpractice crisis. And we conclude the chapter with a broader view of the challenges of continuity and change reflected in an evolving rule of law.

In chapter 3, we explore the lawyer's role as problem solver. We outline the uniqueness of American legal education and explain how this training produces professionals who become society's line drawers. We explicate some of the tasks that lawyers routinely are asked to perform, and we walk readers through a number of the practice areas of law beyond courtroom litigation.

Chapter 4 is the most dense and procedure-focused section of the book. It looks at the safeguards built into the American legal system and highlights the role of the legal profession in protecting citizens' rights. We outline the checks on the system itself, including such controversial subjects as the contingent fee, punitive damages, testimony of expert witnesses, rights of the accused, control of frivolous litigation, roles of the judge and the jury, and the emergence of alternative forms of dispute resolution. We also introduce legal ethical standards as a means of controlling overzealous attorneys and outline the needs and opportunities for future reform.

Chapter 5 contrasts the substantial contributions that lawyers have made in helping create a more just society with the long and growing list of as yet unmet legal needs. The problems we will face in the twenty-first century can barely be envisioned but, no doubt, will require creative legal thought. Lawyers must devise new policies and protections for issues ranging from genetic manipulation to space law. In this chapter, we propose a series of reforms to aid the legal profession in drawing new and different lines that will guide society in these times of change.

Our book concludes with a chapter for those who are thinking of becoming the next generation of America's lawyers. This is something of an atta-girl/boy sermon, one that we hope will help enlist the best and the brightest as future members of our profession.

We intend, through our book, to aid in bringing the public and the legal profession together to ensure that new generations of Americans understand and continue to benefit from the rule of law. Only if law schools continue to attract bright and morally committed students can these historic human legal rights and traditions survive. As we look to defend, reform, and strengthen the legal system, we must not forget to honor and to celebrate. For the United States is a nation in which the rule of law matters. In such a democracy, the lawyer is truly an indispensable professional. Law is a career worthy of the brightest and most dedicated of the forthcoming generations of idealistic and ambitious men and women.

We believe that the story of the legal profession in America is more than lawyer chauvinism. As Winston Churchill said in his defense of the historical reality of King Arthur—it is true, and more, and even better. The long historical contribution of America's lawyers was aptly summarized by Anthony Capozzi, while he served as president of the California Bar Association:

> Despite all of the lawyer negativity, the truth is that in our hours of national crisis, our society has embraced the lawyers and has looked to lawyers for guidance and leadership. An appellate lawyer from Virginia wrote the Declaration of Independence. A trial lawyer, yes trial

lawyer, from Illinois, issued the Emancipation Proclamation. A corporate lawyer from New York led us through the dark hours of the Great Depression and then a world war. And most recently, a trial lawyer, as mayor, led the people of New York through the tragic aftermath of 9/11.

1
LAWYERS ARE ESSENTIAL
IN AMERICAN SOCIETY

as young boys, we were encouraged by our families to become lawyers—not because we were so bright or clever, but because we were argumentative, contesting anything that anyone asserted. We argued all the time, and the side we took didn't much matter to us. Many Americans continue to think of lawyers as Sir Laurence Olivier described actors—the two-year-old who stands in the middle of the room shouting, "Look at me, look at me!"

Robert McKay, longtime dean of New York University School of Law, declared that "lawyers are seldom loved—but often needed." Indeed, he concluded, "in a complex society, expert assistance must be found to cut through the maze of statutes, rules, procedures, government regulations, and private law. Lawyers are trained to perform this important service better than others, and their work is indispensable to the smooth functioning of nearly every aspect of modern life."[1]

The role that the ordinary American lawyer plays in the service of a specific client and of society at large is illustrated by the experience of two little-known Valparaiso University law school graduates. They were called on to represent a young Indiana boy whose name became a household word—a symbol of courage as well as the power of the cooperative spirit under the rule of law.

"Were it not for Charles Vaughan Sr., and his son Charlie," wrote law reporter Kristin Jass Armstrong, "the world might not know the name Ryan White. Sir Elton John would certainly not have sung at his funeral nor would the United States Congress have enacted a Comprehensive AIDS Resource Emergency (CARE) Act in his name. But thanks to the Vaughans' successful representation of the AIDS-stricken Indiana teenager, not only was White able to go to school with his classmates, but the entire nation had its preconceptions about the disease altered."[2]

The story of Ryan White is fairly well known, but the role of his legal representatives is not. It is most beautifully and dramatically understood in the words of the lawyers themselves. Twenty-one years after Ryan was excluded from public schools, Charles Vaughan Sr. recalled the experience:

> I told [Ryan's mother Jeanne] the situation wasn't good but I also said I wasn't interested. . . . I thought she ought to talk to the principal and superintendent to solve the problem. But Jeanne said school officials told

her they knew she was a single mother without the money to fight the decision so there was nothing she could do about it. Well as soon as she said that, I said we would take her case. I thought, "We'll go after them!"

Things had gotten really ugly and one day Jeanne came in and said, "I don't think I can take this anymore. I think I just want to quit."

I looked at Ryan and asked what he wanted to do. Ryan said he didn't want to quit. So I looked at Jeanne and said, "Well, I represent Ryan." I am still amazed by Ryan's spirit. To think that he had the fight to keep going when his mother wanted to quit—that's something.

For nine months the White case was all we did. We went back and forth from federal to state court. It was an adventure like no other. This single case ended classroom discrimination against children with the disease. Can you think of another case with that type of national reper- cussion? Ryan effectively ended the ability of a school sys- tem to keep kids with AIDS out of classrooms. Through Ryan's courage and honesty he helped a nation under- stand what AIDS is—and is not—and how people do and don't get it.[3]

Ryan did that with the help and determination of two un- known lawyers from the small town of Kokomo, Indiana. The Vaughans and the Whites, working within the framework of the American legal system, reshaped the thinking and the actions of a large nation.

The reality of the life and practice of this country's more than one million licensed lawyers differs substantially from the views held by most Americans. A recent study showed that in the minds of the American public, the term "lawyer" was almost synonymous with "courtroom advocate." Lawyers on television, for example, are shown spending 80 percent of their time in the courtroom; for actual, practicing lawyers, that figure is less than 20 percent.[4] In fact, relatively few cases even make it to trial. In 2005, for example, of 2,315 tort actions filed in U.S. district courts, only 149 cases reached trial; of 2,778 civil rights actions filed, only 90 reached trial. In the final analysis of U.S. district court cases terminated during the twelve-month period ending September 30, 2005, only 3,899 of the 270,973 cases filed reached trial.[5]

Lawyers are much more than cinematic courtroom mouthpieces. Data on the legal professions shows a richly diverse practice setting. The American Bar Foundation's *Lawyer Statistical Report* shows the following breakdown:

Table 1. **Practice Setting**

Practice Area	1980 (%)	1991 (%)	2000 (%)
Private practice	68	73	74
Government	9	8	8
Private industry	10	9	8
Retired/inactive	5	5	5
Judiciary	4	3	3
Education	1	1	1
Legal aid/public defender	2	1	1
Private association	1	1	1

Note: Totals may not add up to 100 percent because of rounding.

Sources: Adapted from a compilation by the ABA Market Research Department, "Lawyer Demographics," http://www.abanet.org/marketresearch/lawyer _demographics_2006.pdf. The underlying statistics are drawn from American Bar Foundation, *The Lawyer Statistical Report*, 1985, 1994, and 2004 editions.

Professor Ferdinand Stone, in his classic *Handbook of Law Study*, summarizes what most lawyers do:

> In our society [lawyers] perform many functions. They are the counselors and advisors in matters of business, in family affairs, and in government; in short, in whatever realm of activities the law teaches. They are the planners in such matters as the disposition of their estates during life and after death, the employment of their funds, and the organization of their personal and business ventures. Lawyers are called upon to draft legislation, ordinances, or by-laws which govern a corporation or society. These are the general functions of the lawyer.[6]

The general public's perception of what lawyers do is incomplete. Critics of the legal profession tend to focus on a very narrow range of courtroom lawyering, mostly personal injury and criminal defense. The truer range of lawyerly tasks is reflected in the job description that Peanuts cartoonist Charles M. Schulz created for Snoopy in *See You Later, Litigator*. When asked his specialization, the lawyer-dog hands over his business card, which proclaims: "Bankruptcy, trusts, accidents, medical, probate, wills, and DOG BITES."[7]

Lawrence Friedman, the Stanford legal historian, provides a scholarly overview of the working world of the twenty-first-century lawyer.

> Overwhelmingly lawyers manage business affairs. Small firms work for small businesses, large firms work for large businesses. Some firms also handle enormous "deals," mergers of billion-dollar corporations, and

mega-transactions in which one colossus swallows up another one. A giant economy—an economy measured in trillions, not billions—is an economy that generates deals, mergers, incorporations, buyouts; it is an economy with huge antitrust suits, huge tort actions, class action cases that last for years and call for whole armies of attorneys, patent and copyright matters on which the fate of industries rest, and so on endlessly. It is an economy that floats on a sea of lawyers.[8]

We sometimes forget that substantial numbers of law-trained individuals do not engage in the traditional practice of law. For example, at one time the commissioner of every single professional sport was a lawyer. Many more lawyers serve as CEOs or operational officers of companies, large and small. They edit books and magazines, serve as literary and theatrical agents, and publish newspapers. The editor of the *New York Times* crossword puzzles was a lawyer by training. Increasingly, law schools are discovering at class reunions that from 30 to 50 percent of their graduates are working in areas in which their law training has prepared them for nontraditional jobs. A recent *New Yorker* cartoon shows a "lawyer slash filmmaker," "lawyer slash actor," and "lawyer slash playwright."[9] And, of course, lawyers as politicians, legislators, and government administrators are legion.

The vast majority of the nation's lawyers are not trial lawyers. They are not Johnny Cochran or Clarence Darrow. In fact, much of the typical lawyer's practice is so-called preventative law. Most of this day-to-day lawyering is so ordinary and dull that novelists and filmmakers pass it by. Roger Ebert, the Pulitzer Prize–winning film critic, concluded that "nothing could be more boring than an absolutely accurate movie about law."[10] What most lawyers do is think things through—they try to anticipate the legal pitfalls of a particular course of action. Then they advise the client on how to avoid those pitfalls or how to meet them, should they, in fact, occur.

There are many different lives among America's million-plus lawyers. James G. Leipold, executive director of the National Association for Law Placement (NALP), reported to law school deans that although more than 90 percent of law school graduates had found employment in the profession six months after graduation, there was no single career path.[11] He noted, for example, that there are two major divisions—almost two separate professions. The relatively few lawyers starting in large, elite corporate firms in cities like Los Angeles, New York, Chicago, and Washington, D.C., receive a median salary of $125,000, with $160,000 the current high. Median starting salary for all private firms is only $67,000. Those employed in the public sector are starting as low as $36,000, and the median for all these lawyers, such as public defenders and states attorneys (including experienced practitioners), is about $45,000. For state government lawyers, the median is $40,000, and for the federal government lawyers, the number is $53,000. The popular concept of the fat-cat lawyer made rich by runaway medical malpractice and product liability cases is not borne out by the facts. Indeed, when the high level of law student debt is factored into the equation, the image is simply wrong—and dramatically wrong! Each year, despite these data, some 125,000 to 140,000 students enroll in law schools, preparing for the challenges and opportunities of a legal career. About 20 percent of these new law students are minorities, and 50 percent are women.

Every year in late summer and early fall, law school deans and incoming legal neophytes participate in the historic rite of passage called "new law student orientation." This ritual has been described as a combination of the Veiled Prophet's debutante ball and a New Guinea circumcision ceremony. At this time, the grizzled old dean or, with increasing frequency, the bright young dean begins the professional indoctrination of a new generation of America's lawyers. Deans' orientation speeches are as different as law school deans themselves. Ours certainly were. And law school deans, like the rest of the legal profession, are an increasingly diverse lot of women and men from varied social, ethnic, and religious backgrounds. These deans' addresses have at least one thing in common: They are intended to set new servants of the law on the high road with an elevated view of what law and lawyers can and should do for society.

This rite of passage, like all forms of professional indoctrination, involves the invocation of heroes from Edward Coke to Thomas More to Abraham Lincoln to Thurgood Marshall and Sandra Day O'Connor. Each of these lives tells a story of struggle and virtue, of crisis and contribution. Generally missing from these orientation sessions is the parallel portrayal of the dark side of the lawyer in folk proverbs and poetic verse, not to mention lawyer jokes, shaggy dog stories, cartoons, and political rhetoric. Each of these negative images also tells a story that would-be attorneys need to know. These professional cautionary tales raise the question, "If lawyers are such heroes, then why are lawyers the butt of jokes and the object of thousands of years of love-hate relationships?" Why did Carl Sandburg write that the horse drawing the funeral hearse of a lawyer always has a smile, or Shakespeare have a minor figure shout, "Kill all the lawyers," or Dickens proclaim, "Then, Sir, the law is a ass, a idiot"? The answer is relatively simple. In a nation so law-focused and with such pervasive economic and social regulation, lawyers have immense power. This kind of lawyer power, access, and control is deeply resented. Citizens feel beaten down by law—or too many laws and too much change. If what most lawyers did was defend Santa Claus, as in the film *Miracle on 34th Street* (1947), then the national sense of humor and outrage might be focused on other professionals.

In our days of law school deaning, we admit that we approached orientation—the task of initially defining law, lawyers, and lawyering—from opposite directions. One of us began his speech with a parable from Senate chaplain Peter Marshall; the other liked to start out with General George Patton's most famous speech delivered to his troops just before battle. Each orientation story illustrates different views and challenges of lawyering.

We both included Abraham Lincoln as the heroic model in describing the role of law and lawyering in American democracy. Back in 1837, long before he became a national figure, young Abe—just beginning his legendary lawyering career—spoke of the significance and centrality of law in American life. He called for a strong public commitment to law in an address to the Young Men's Lyceum in Springfield, Illinois:

> Let reverence for the laws be breathed by every American mother to the lisping babe that prattles on her lap; let it be taught in schools, in seminaries, and in colleges; let it be written in primers, spelling-books, and in almanacs; let it be preached from the pulpit, proclaimed in legislative halls, and enforced in courts of justice. And, in short, let it become the political religion of the nation; and let the old and the young, the rich and the poor, the grave and the gay of all sexes and tongues and colors and conditions, sacrifice increasingly upon its altars.[12]

The power of the rule of law in American democracy is not a quaint Lincolnesque remnant or dated nineteenth-century concept. In fact, the argument proclaiming the primacy of law resonates even more strongly in the twenty-first century. Two twentieth-century U.S. presidents—both nonlawyers—set forth the case most ably. "Certain other societies," John F. Kennedy proclaimed, "may respect the rule of force—we respect the rule of law." His successor, Lyndon B. Johnson, was even more focused: "[Law] liberates the desire to build and subdues the desire to destroy. And if war can tear us apart, law can unite us—out of fear, or love, or reason, or all three. Law is the greatest human invention. All the rest give man mastery over his world. Law gives him mastery over himself."[13]

In our first-year orientation speeches, both of us try to spell out the beauty and the majesty of the law as well as to explain what lawyers do. We attempt to describe the lawyer's role in a democratic society. We do this by analogy and example, drawing upon descriptions and experiences from many people.

There is no more vivid or inspiring picture than this one borrowed from Peter Marshall, the Scottish-born chaplain of the U.S. Senate in the years following the Second World War. Marshall offered the parable of the Keeper of the Springs at a time (not unlike the present) when lawyers and judges faced the challenge of balancing domestic and foreign threats with preserving constitutional and human rights.[14] The Marshall parable is set forth below:

> Once upon a time, a certain town grew up at the foot of a mountain range.
>
> High up in the hills, a strange and quiet forest dweller took it upon himself to be the Keeper of the Springs.

He patrolled the hills and wherever he found a spring he cleaned its brown pool of silt and fallen leaves, of mud and mould, and took away from the spring all foreign matter, so that the water which bubbled up through the sand ran down clean and cold and pure.

It leaped sparkling over rocks and dropped joyously in crystal cascades until, swollen by other streams, it became a river of life to the busy town.

Millwheels were whirled by its rush.

Gardens were refreshed by its waters.

Fountains threw it like diamonds into the air.

Swans sailed on its limpid surface, and children laughed as they played on its banks in the sunshine.

But the City Council was a group of hard-headed, hard-boiled business men. They scanned the civic budget and found in it the salary of a Keeper of the Springs.

Said the Keeper of the Purse: "Why should we pay this romance ranger? We never see him; he is not necessary to our town's work life. If we build a reservoir just above the town, we can dispense with his services and save his salary."

Therefore, the City Council voted to dispense with the unnecessary cost of a Keeper of the Springs, and to build a cement reservoir.

So the Keeper of the Springs no longer visited the brown pools but watched from the heights while they built the reservoir.

When it was finished it soon filled up with water to be sure but the water did not seem to be the same.

It did not seem to be as clean, and a green scum soon befouled its stagnant surface.

Lawyers Are Essential

There were constant troubles with the delicate machinery of the mills, for it was often clogged with slime, and the swans found another home above the town.

At last an epidemic raged and the clammy, yellow fingers of sickness reached into every home in every street and lane.

The City Council met again. Sorrowfully it faced the city's plight and frankly it acknowledged the mistake of the dismissal of the Keeper of the Springs.

They sought him out in his hermit hut high in the hills and begged him to return to his former joyous labor.

Gladly he agreed and began once more to make his rounds.

It was not long until pure water came lilting down under tunnels of ferns and mosses and to sparkle in the cleansed reservoir.

Millwheels turned again as of old.

Stenches disappeared.

Sickness waned, and convalescent children playing in the sun laughed again because the swans had come back.

The moral of this parable, first used by Marshall for a Mother's Day sermon, is that we take for granted individuals and institutions that work. Because they work so well, they often seem unnecessary, costly, and even troublesome. We cannot imagine what would befall us without their continued presence. The current attack on lawyers, judges, and the legal profession is such a case. Many of the specific concerns and complaints may be justified. Nonetheless, American lawyers and judges are underappreciated and misunderstood. Their influence is, as the

French social observer Alexis de Tocqueville noted, "the most powerful existing security against the excesses of democracy."[15]

The other dean regularly began his orientation speech by screening a minute or so from the opening address of General George Patton to his troops in the movie *Patton* (1970). After seeing this brief clip, the would-be lawyers are told that they are enlisting for service in support of the betterment of society and that, indeed, "lawyers are the foot soldiers of our Constitution."

Every day, in courtrooms throughout the land, our nation's lawyers, representing all sides of civil cases and criminal prosecutions as well as economic development issues, fight to preserve basic human, economic, and constitutional rights. They demand factual accuracy, procedural fairness, and decisions that are based on neutral, informed fact-finding. In all controversies, especially legal ones, there are winners and losers—what is important is that decisions are made openly, based on neutral principles of law that preserve human dignity and protect democratic processes. And whom do we enlist to do this job? Our lawyers.

The two authors, despite our divergent orientation presentations of a Senate chaplain and an army general, introduced new law students to the ideal of the ennobling professional life lived by the humanistic lawyer. In describing this possibility, we both quote Oliver Wendell Holmes Jr., who asks:

> How can the laborious study of a dry and technical system, the greedy watch for clients and practice of shopkeepers' arts, the mannerless conflicts over sordid interests, make out a life? . . . If a man has the soul of Sancho Panza, the world to him will be Sancho Panza's world; but if he has the soul of an idealist, he will make—I do not say find—his world ideal. Of course, the law is not the place

Lawyers Are Essential

for the artist or the poet. The law is the calling of thinkers. But to those who believe with me that not the least god-like of man's activities is the large survey of causes, that to know is not less than to feel, I say—and I say no longer with any doubt—that man [or woman] may live greatly in the law as well as elsewhere; that there as well as elsewhere his thought may find its unity in an infinite perspective; that there as well as elsewhere he may wreak himself upon life, may drink the bitter cup of heroism, may wear his heart out after the unattainable.[16]

Our nation's founders established in the U.S. Constitution the guiding principles for the oldest continuing democracy on the face of the globe. Since we ratified the Constitution in 1789, all other developed nations have undergone governmental up-heavals that drastically changed their form of government. Our founders—most of them law-trained—gave birth to the stunning new notion that the people could form a more perfect union by checking and balancing government powers while protecting the fundamental rights of each citizen. Since that time, the individuals to whom these rights apply have been dramatically expanded. And this expansion, including women, African Americans, and other minorities, is—in significant ways—the result of the work of America's lawyers. Those lofty notions of the Constitution would very soon have become hollow paper promises without a strong, vigilant, independent legal profession and judiciary.

Before the collapse of the USSR, the old Soviet constitution contained many more guarantees than our Bill of Rights—and those rights were unenforced, ignored, cynically proclaimed, and regularly abandoned. Soviet judges were pawns of that state; lawyers were employee-handmaidens of that same state. Both Soviet lawyers and judges understood that their first duty was to the state—not to the individual client or to the broader values of the people. Our Bill of Rights flourishes, in large part, because our lawyers are independent and because our judges have the duty of measuring all our laws against constitutional guarantees rooted in human rights and values. The old Soviet lawyers could never be viewed as constitutional foot soldiers or keepers of their springs. The waters of their legal system became foul and corrupted and ultimately ceased to flow. American lawyers are constantly involved in settling disputes, evolving new principles, and helping purify the legal springs that keep democracy's waters fresh and flowing. This reality of the lawyer's role contrasts with the popular lawyer joke that asks, "How are beavers like lawyers?" Answer: "They both dam up the works!"[17]

Toward the middle of the twentieth century, Yale law professor Fred Rodell's indictment of the power of lawyers began thus:

> In tribal times, there were the medicine-men. In the middle ages, there were priests. Today there are the lawyers. For every age, [there is] a group of bright boys [the correct gender identification of most lawyers when Rodell was writing in 1939], learned in their trade and jealous of their learning, who blend technical competence with plain and fancy hocus-pocus to make themselves masters of their fellow men. For every age, [there is] a pseudo-intellectual autocracy, guarding the tricks of this trade from the uninitiated, and running, after its own pattern, the civilization of its day.
>
> It is the lawyers who run our civilization for us—our governments, our business, our private lives. Most legislators are lawyers; they make our laws. Most presidents,

Lawyers Are Essential

governors, commissioners, along with their advisers and brain-trusts are lawyers; they administer our laws. All the judges are lawyers; they interpret and enforce our laws. There is no separation of powers where the lawyers are concerned. There is only a concentration of all government power—in the lawyers. As the school boy put it, ours is "a government of lawyers, not men."[18]

Today, it might be hard to find anyone willing to argue with Rodell about the power of lawyers. This pervasive power is, no doubt, one of the chief reasons for popular resentment against the profession. At the same time, we Americans have a particularly long and historic sense of the rule of law and lawyers in our civilization. The relationship has been an ambiguous one, at best love-hate. In our earliest history, some colonial statutes, for example, prohibited the practice of law and outlawed attorneys.[19] But always, always, regardless of the prevailing attitude toward lawyers, there has been a sense that this is a nation of laws. The invocation of the rule of law is more American than apple or cherry pie. Law and lawyers have always been at the center of American civilization.

This historic centrality, ambiguity, and hostility is reflected in the influential nineteenth-century *McGuffey's Eclectic Readers*. In the *Third Reader*, Mr. Barlow, a colonist, invented a play for his children in which "people of different trades and professions" offer themselves to go with him to found a new world colony. The lawyer's plea to join the expedition is rejected. "Sir . . . when we are rich enough to go to law, we will let you know," the colonist replies, as he turns away the lawyer.[20] Rarely are McGuffey's lawyers favorably portrayed; generally, they are depicted as "being more self-serving" and "their motives . . . nearly always suspect."[21]

Today, as one drives about America's countryside, one encounters courthouses in the same way that cathedrals dot the European backcountry. This is a reminder of the significance of law in America's pioneer life. Almost without exception, the courthouse is in the center of things, at least geographically. It sits in the heart of the community, in what we have come to call "the courthouse square." A nineteenth-century farm boy who became a very successful small-town lawyer contended that he made that career choice because as a little boy, when his family came from the farm into the tiny Carolina county seat, he could run to the courthouse and visit the lawyers. As he recalled, "In the summer they would be sitting on the lawn eating watermelon and in the winter they would be standing before red-hot pot-bellied stoves making great speeches." And that was what he decided he wanted to do with his life—eat watermelon and make speeches.[22]

This was not just the isolated view of an impressionable farm boy. The majesty of the law was the most frequent theme of nineteenth-century Fourth of July picnic orations, and lawyers were most generally the orators. We sometimes forget that the great patriotic hymn to our national chauvinism, "America the Beautiful," includes the lines "Confirm thy soul in self-control / Thy liberty in law." Americans have always seen a strong connection between liberty and law. Perhaps we have romanticized the role of the written law, but there is no question that it is the cornerstone of our perceived guarantees of individual liberty. We, as a people, believe in the rule of law.

In an earlier America, law provided much of the public diversion—indeed, entertainment. In the Massachusetts Bay Colony, where almost every form of public or personal pleasure was prohibited, the law was open and regularly used almost as a public sport. Law was the true-life *Survivor, West Wing,* and *American Idol* of the western settlement experience. Trials and hangings and the arguments of lawyers on court day drew immense crowds. The jury was often spoken of as "the law school of the masses," and one Ozark pioneer recalled, "[F]rom the time I became twenty-one years old, I don't suppose I missed a year of some court a-bein' on the jury, till they thought I got too old to know right from wrong."[23]

As if they could not get enough of it, groups of neighbors gathered at schoolhouse pie suppers and Arbor Day picnics to hold humorous kangaroo courts at which locals played judge and lawyer, trying their friends on such trumped-up charges as "stealing watermelons" or "keeping company with a girl too long without askin' her to marry." Out in Rock Creek, Nebraska, the literary society met on the night of January 27, 1882, to debate the question "Resolved: That Lawyers Are a Public Nuisance." By a decision of two votes to one, the judges found for the negative.[24]

As the pragmatic response of our frontier settlers indicates, characterizations of lawyers and their role in American society are not limited to the noblest issues of constitutional rights or civic virtues. In addition to being keepers of the springs, foot soldiers of the Constitution, and stewards of democracy, lawyers are also architects of commerce and carpenters of business. Lawyers are major figures in the creation of the instruments and transactions that keep business and the economy afloat and help produce prosperity.

The American people themselves see lawyers and the law from many angles—some positive, others negative. It is almost as if the legal system were a giant kaleidoscope of limitless pieces, shifting colors and design depending upon how it is moved, from which side it is viewed, and who is looking. In explaining this diverse legal system to undergraduate classes at Stanford, the distinguished legal historian Lawrence Friedman made the following comparison:

> The legal system is something like the bridge. The bridge itself was not "autonomous"; it was entirely the product of a social demand. But once in place it began to exert an influence on behavior and on attitudes. . . . They ordered their lives in reference to the bridge. The bridge entered into their very thought process. American law is very much of this nature: it is one of society's bridges.[25]

Using Friedman's analysis, one might speak of lawyers as bridge builders—although newspaper columnist Jane Bryant Quinn sees Friedman's bridge in a slightly different light. To her, "Lawyers are operators of toll bridges which anyone in search of justice must pass."[26]

A group of reform-minded attorneys and judges has described lawyers as "healers of the body politic." Of course, this concept of the lawyer is not new. Abe Lincoln urged that being "a peacemaker [gave] the lawyer a superior opportunity of being a good man."[27] Among the ancients, Epictetus concluded, "As physicians are the preservers of the sick, so are [lawyers] of the injured."[28] Chief Justice Warren Burger, in comparing doctors and lawyers, suggested that physicians "still retain a high degree of public confidence because they are perceived as healers." The chief justice then issued a challenge to the legal profession. "Should lawyers not be healers! Healers, not warriors. Healers, not procurers. Healers, not hired guns."[29] The American Bar Association has taken up that cry, and today many local, state, and national leaders of the profession focus on the lawyer's role in legal healing.

Television comic Jerry Seinfeld wryly observed, "To me, a lawyer is basically the person who knows the rules of the country. We're all throwing the dice, playing the game, moving our pieces around the board, but if there is a problem, the lawyer is the only person who read the inside of the top of the box."[30] And Seinfeld got it right! Law is everywhere. Whether seen in the directions on the stand-up comic's mythical game of life or in the heroic murals in the marble rotunda of a great courthouse, law relates to everything the ordinary citizen does. The law casts a long and majestic shadow. Law is the basis of liberty, justice, and fairness as well as the controlling instrument of economic, political, and social forces. From public utility districts to zoning boards, from the safety of our children's toys to the security of our national airports, from protecting the environment to establishing the conditions and hours of our work life, law dominates and dictates, even impinges. And in the final analysis, the ability to cope often depends upon lawyers. One's ability to comply, to change—even to survive—rests with lawyers. In a sense, in this society, the lawyer is the everywhere man. He is not only Seinfeld's "person who read the inside of the top of the box" but also most likely the person who wrote the instructions in the first place.

MYTHS AND MISUNDERSTANDINGS
ABOUT AMERICAN LAW AND LAWYERS

S ocial scientists and popular folklorists often write about urban legends and myths. These include such diverse topics as spiders in the hairdo, alligators in the New York sewers, and runaway lawsuits. In this chapter, we explore a range of law- and lawyer-related myths as well as common misunderstandings about how the legal system operates.

Are There Too Many Lawyers?

It is a fact that there are now more than one million licensed lawyers in the United States. When the lighted ball descended on Times Square on December 31, 2006, the official number was 1,116,967.[1] From this point of fact, critics of the legal system have fashioned the conclusion that there are too many lawyers, an assertion heard frequently and one that goes almost unchallenged. To the uninformed, the raw numbers seem to confirm the statement—yes, there must surely be too many. Yet such a conclusion is profoundly untrue.[2] There are not too many lawyers produced by American law schools. Data from the National Association of Law Placement refute that assumption, actually showing a demand for *more* trained lawyers.[3] The following charts show the distribution of lawyers in the United States by age, sex, ethnicity, location, firm association, and governmental or private area of specialization as well as the number of enrolled law students. These are not members of a monolithic, undifferentiated class of "lawyers." They represent individuals of varied backgrounds engaged in a wide range of pursuits.

One common response of critics is that other countries get by on fewer lawyers—Japan is often cited as a prime example. The Great Japanese Lawyer Myth was widely proclaimed by former vice president Dan Quayle. In point of fact, Japan may have more *law-trained persons* per capita than the United States. The trick is that the Japanese system defines the term "lawyer" far more narrowly than the American system does. Here are the facts behind the myth:

- In Japan, as in most countries, law is an *undergraduate* discipline. Only in the United States and Canada is law a graduate discipline requiring an undergraduate degree prior to enrollment in law school.

- In Japan, a great many undergraduates major in law. Graduates from these programs use their law

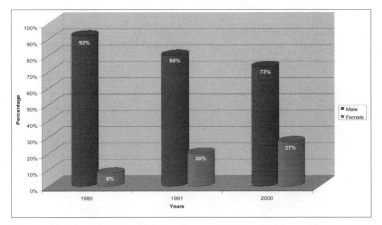

Fig. 2.1. Number of licensed lawyers by sex, 1980–2000. Adapted from a compilation by the ABA Market Research Department, "Lawyer Demographics," http://www.abanet.org/marketresearch/lawyer_demographics_2006.pdf. The underlying statistics are drawn from American Bar Foundation, *The Lawyer Statistical Report,* 1985, 1994, and 2004 editions.

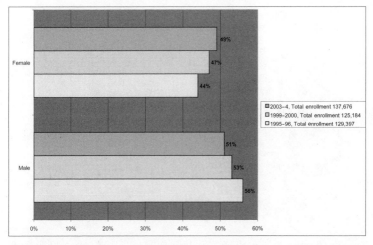

Fig. 2.2. Number of law students by sex, 1995–2004. Adapted from a compilation by the ABA Section of Legal Education and Admission to the Bar, "First Year and Total J.D. enrollment by Gender," http://www.abanet.org/legaled/statistics/charts/stats%20-%206.pdf.

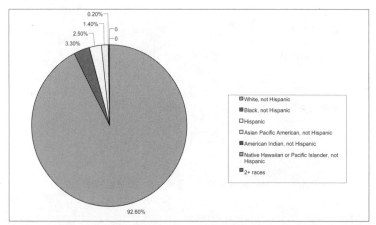

Fig. 2.3. Number of licensed lawyers by race or ethnicity, 1990. Adapted from a compilation by the ABA Market Research Department, "Lawyer Demographics," http://www.abanet.org/marketresearch/lawyer_demographics_2006.pdf. The underlying statistics are drawn from American Bar Foundation, *The Lawyer Statistical Report*, 1985, 1994, and 2004 editions.

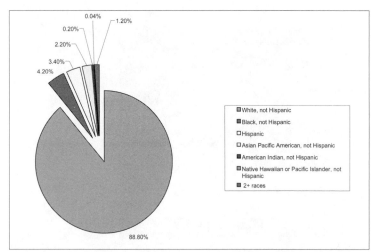

Fig. 2.4. Number of licensed lawyers by race or ethnicity, 2000. Adapted from a compilation by the ABA Market Research Department, "Lawyer Demographics," http://www.abanet.org/marketresearch/lawyer_demographics_2006.pdf. The underlying statistics are drawn from American Bar Foundation, *The Lawyer Statistical Report*, 1985, 1994, and 2004 editions.

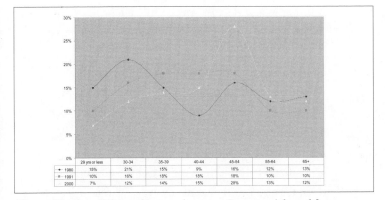

	29 yrs or less	30-34	35-39	40-44	45-54	55-64	65+
1980	15%	21%	15%	9%	16%	12%	13%
1991	10%	16%	18%	18%	18%	10%	10%
2000	7%	12%	14%	15%	28%	13%	12%

Fig. 2.5. Number of licensed lawyers by age, 1980–2000. Adapted from a compilation by the ABA Market Research Department, "Lawyer Demographics," http://www.abanet.org/marketresearch/lawyer_demographics_2006.pdf. The underlying statistics are drawn from American Bar Foundation, *The Lawyer Statistical Report*, 1985, 1994, and 2004 editions.

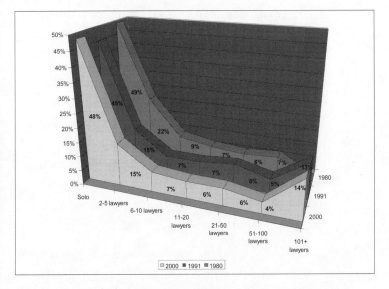

Fig. 2.6. Number of licensed lawyers in private practice by firm size, 1980–2000. Adapted from a compilation by the ABA Market Research Department, "Lawyer Demographics," http://www.abanet.org/marketresearch/lawyer _demographics_2006.pdf. The underlying statistics are drawn from American Bar Foundation, *The Lawyer Statistical Report*, 1985, 1994, and 2004 editions.

training in a variety of ways. Only a few go on to be licensed to practice before the High Court of Japan. These few are the only ones who are officially called "lawyers." The vast majority of graduates who are law-trained are, in fact, involved in law-related employment and focus their careers on legal issues. Most of them do exactly what U.S. lawyers do. For example, in Japan there is a specialized tribunal that resolves housing rental disputes and another that resolves car repair disputes. Those who work in these areas are engaged in what we in America would call the practice of law. They are, for all purposes, lawyers. They are clearly involved in legal dispute resolution. Yet, in Japan, they are not called lawyers or counted in the lawyer census. If they were in the United States, they would be called lawyers.

- Today, Japan is growing concerned about the quality of its legal training programs and is beginning to adopt the U.S. model of graduate legal education— Japan actually wants to *increase* substantially the number of those licensed to practice law before the High Court. As the Japanese economy has grown more sophisticated, the demand for American-style lawyering has grown as well.[4]

Despite the hard data to the contrary, the myth of too many lawyers persists. An old *New Yorker* cartoon pictures a hospital nursery filled with new babies. The doctor announces to the babies born on that particular day, "Attention please. In twenty-five years at 8:45 a.m. on Tuesday, July 29 . . . , you are scheduled to take the New York State bar exam."[5] Despite the popular humor, by the time these babies take their bar exam, there may be too few lawyers both in the United States and in Japan.

In fact, politicians and antilawyer advocates have gotten carried away in asserting that the United States has the vast majority of the world's lawyers. They wildly proclaim that 70 or 80 or even 90 percent of all lawyers are in the United States. Not so! Marc Galanter, of the University of Wisconsin, suggests that the accurate figure is somewhere between one-quarter and one-third of the world's lawyers work in the United States.[6] It should be noted that these numbers correspond to the United States' approximate share of the total goods and services produced in the world each year.

Are There Too Many Lawsuits?

A related myth asserts that in the United States too many lawyers produce too many lawsuits. Claims about America's "hair-trigger litigiousness," as Deborah Rhode, of Stanford, and David Luber, of Georgetown, have concluded, are greatly exaggerated. In fact, historians have observed that many communities in the United States had a higher per capita rate of litigation during the eighteenth and nineteenth centuries. Furthermore, the number of court filings in such countries as Australia, Canada, Denmark, England, Israel, and New Zealand is comparable to that in the United States on a per capita basis.[7]

The small fraction of disputes that actually go to formal legal resolution (the trial process itself) attract media attention and public interest vastly disproportionate to their actual number and frequency. In 2003, the approximately one million civil cases considered by the state and federal court systems were resolved in the following manner:

- 70 percent—dropped or dismissed

- 24 percent—settled

- 5 percent—jury verdict for the defense

- 1 percent—jury verdict for plaintiff[8]

These figures confirm that trials in American courts are becoming less and less frequent—exactly the opposite of what former vice president Quayle and company have touted. Over the last forty years, as the number of lawyers graduating from law school has increased, the percentage of cases going to trial actually has decreased. In the mid-1960s, more than 11 percent of civil cases in federal court were resolved by trials. In the first decade of the twenty-first century, that number is less than 2 percent. The number of federal criminal trials dropped by one-third during that same forty years, and this in spite of the increase in arrests and indictments under the so-called War on Drugs. On average, federal judges who once heard about forty trials per year are now presiding over fewer than nineteen.[9]

Society needs to look at the hard data—to look beyond the surface allegations and into the complexities of modern medicine, the operation of the court system, and the challenges of systematic risk management. The data are clear. The following two graphs represent the number of federal civil cases that were filed, were settled before trial, or went to trial within a one-year period beginning September 30, 2004.[10] Figure 2.7 depicts the 270,973 civil cases filed in the U.S. district courts. Although some court action occurred in 208,312 of those cases, only 3,899 ever reached trial. The others were resolved before pretrial, during pretrial, or after pretrial. In short, only 1.4 percent of the total number of civil cases filed in the federal courts were ever tried. This

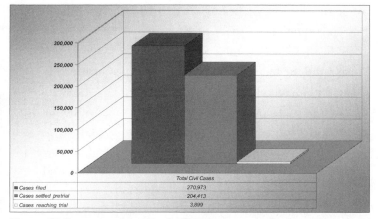

	Total Civil Cases
■ Cases filed	270,973
■ Cases settled pretrial	204,413
□ Cases reaching trial	3,899

Fig. 2.7. Civil cases terminated in the U.S. district courts for the twelve-month period ending September 30, 2005. Adapted from Leonidas Ralph Mecham, *Judicial Business of the United States Courts: 2005 Report of the Director,* table C-4, http://www.uscourts.gov/judbus2005/appendices/c4.pdf.

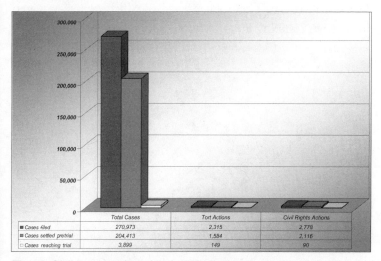

	Total Cases	Tort Actions	Civil Rights Actions
■ Cases filed	270,973	2,315	2,778
■ Cases settled pretrial	204,413	1,584	2,116
□ Cases reaching trial	3,899	149	90

Fig. 2.8. Civil cases terminated in the U.S. district courts, with torts and civil rights actions as proportion of the total, for the twelve-month period ending September 30, 2005. Adapted from Leonidas Ralph Mecham, *Judicial Business of the United States Courts: 2005 Report of the Director,* table C-4, http://www.uscourts.gov/judbus2005/appendices/c4.pdf.

astoundingly low number differs dramatically from the chronic misrepresentations of the media.

To further illustrate the discrepancy between media representations and the facts, two important case classifications demonstrate the low numbers. Figure 2.8 depicts the total number of tort actions (suits for redress of a private wrong) within the overall total of civil cases. Actions were filed in 2,315 tort cases for the year, which included marine personal injury, motor vehicle personal injury, other personal injury, and other assorted torts. Once again, a large majority—1,584 of those cases—were concluded in pretrial: only 149 of the 2,315 actions filed ever reached trial. This number hardly suggests a bursting of the floodgates of justice.

Figure 2.9 depicts the number of civil rights actions filed in U.S. district courts. They totaled 2,778, of which 2,116 terminated in pretrial, resulting in a paltry 90 cases reaching trial. Clearly,

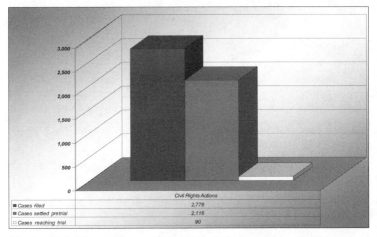

	Civil Rights Actions
■ Cases filed	2,778
■ Cases settled pretrial	2,116
□ Cases reaching trial	90

Fig. 2.9. Civil rights actions terminated in the U.S. district courts for the twelve-month period ending September 30, 2005. Adapted from Leonidas Ralph Mecham, *Judicial Business of the United States Courts: 2005 Report of the Director*, table C-4, http://www.uscourts.gov/judbu2005/appendices/c4.pdf.

the media attention to lawsuits vastly misrepresents the modern legal landscape.

Is There Too Much Law?

While it is true that the United States has a substantial lawyer-to-nonlawyer ratio, the United States also has a most sophisticated economy, one of the highest standards of living, and, despite recent antiterrorist measures, among the highest levels of human rights protection of any nation in the world. Not only is the need for lawyers substantially greater than the supply, but legal reform and promulgation of appropriate regulations frequently cannot keep up with our rapidly changing society. Furthermore, there are many areas—particularly rural pockets, minority districts, small towns, and inner-city zones—where legal needs are woefully underserved. There are also many sophisticated new techniques for committing fraud or enriching the few, and the regulators can't keep up. America's problem is not too many lawyers, and it is not overregulation; it is, rather, a serious problem with the distribution of legal talent. Many lawyers remain in small college towns, while others gravitate to major population centers or more lucrative practice areas. But even in large cities with substantial numbers of lawyers, many citizens lack resources to attend to their serious legal problems. The real issue that needs to be addressed is the adequate funding of the legal system so that these needs can be met. In short, more, not less, legal help is needed.

The system is slowly beginning to correct itself through legal aid, law outreach programs, and prepaid legal services. Delivery of legal services is an area in which there is need for substantial reform. Legal talent needs to be better distributed and more

Myths and Misunderstandings

effectively utilized. Former president Jimmy Carter, never known as a friend of lawyers, clearly identified the heart of the distribution issue: "No resource . . . in our society . . . is more wastefully or unfairly distributed than legal skills [when] ninety percent of our lawyers serve 10% of our people."[11] Serious studies suggest that as few as 20 percent of American citizens have their legal needs fully met.[12]

There are examples, however, of success in increasing the number of lawyers to help meet specialized legal needs that previously had gone unfulfilled. Perhaps the best example deals with the American Indian.[13] Much of the recent improvement in Native American communities over the last two decades, especially in the protection of tribal sovereign rights, is a result of increasing the number of Indian lawyers. That, in turn, is primarily the product of the Pre-Law Summer Institute of the American Indian Law Center at the University of New Mexico. A dynamic combination of law-trained Native people, such as Robert Bennett and P. Sam Deloria, and non-Indian legal educators, such as former University of New Mexico dean Fred Hart, envisioned what more Indian lawyers could do to help meet the needs of tribal people. And they did something about it.

Beginning with only a handful of Native lawyers at the beginning of the 1970s, this program, working with law schools, bar associations, private foundations, government agencies, and tribal entities, has helped shepherd the education of more than two thousand law-trained Natives who now work for tribes, firms, governments, schools, Indian businesses, and private industry. These briefcase warriors have, through lawsuits and negotiations on issues as varied as gaming and fishing rights, quite literally, brought a legal and economic revolution to many parts of Indian country.

Are Lawsuits Necessarily a Bad Thing?

Another myth is that any change in law that results in an increase in lawsuits is always a bad thing. Nothing could be further from the truth. A change in law that better protects citizens' rights or provides better access to the courts can be a very good thing, even if it increases the number of suits filed. A case in point is the famous decision of Justice Benjamin Cardozo in *MacPherson v. Buick Motor Co.*[14] The case was decided by the New York Court of Appeals, the state's highest court, in 1916. At the time, automobiles were being mass-produced, and their use was rapidly growing. Not surprisingly, the number of automobile accidents causing serious injuries and deaths was also increasing, and many of those accidents were the result of faulty parts or bad design. Under the common law of that time, however, those injured by defective vehicles could not recover damages against the manufacturer, however egregious the fault. Recovery was blocked by legal precedent decided in an earlier and very different age, which held that if a manufacturer assembled a defective vehicle, the company could not be found liable for injuries to the ultimate consumer or user of the product. Why?

Buick assembled a car with a defective wooden wheel purchased from a different manufacturer. Buick could have detected that the wheel was defective by a careful examination of the part; unfortunately, it did not. Buick sold the defective vehicle to a dealer, and the dealer sold it to MacPherson. While the car was in motion, one of the wooden spokes "crumbled into fragments," and MacPherson was injured when he was thrown from the car. MacPherson sued Buick for negligence in its failure to properly inspect the vehicle. Buick claimed that it owed no duty to the ultimate purchaser of the car, citing old English precedent that had become well established in American case law. Buick argued that the plaintiff, MacPherson, lacked "privity of contract" with it as the manufacturer. Simply put, Buick's contract was with the dealer; the ultimate purchaser was a "legal stranger" to Buick.

This old doctrine requiring privity of contract to recover for damages was cut down by Justice Cardozo's opinion. He wrote that the suit was a simple negligence action that should not be barred by ancient contract doctrine. Buick knew that the cars it manufactured and sold to dealers would then be sold by those dealers to customers. Buick could readily foresee that a defective car could cause injury and damage to the ultimate user. By this reasoning, Buick had a duty to the ultimate user of its product. Its failure to properly inspect this vehicle breached that duty, resulting in MacPherson's injury. Buick was therefore liable for the resulting damages.

As simple and unremarkable as the case seems today, it ushered in the development of modern product liability law that has protected literally millions. In the decades after Justice Cardozo's opinion, there emerged a general rule that imposes liability on all sellers of defective products—regardless of whether the claim is for personal injury or property damage, whether the manufacturer produced the whole product or a significant component part, or whether the person injured was the immediate purchaser or not. Did *MacPherson v. Buick Motor Co.* and its progeny cause more lawsuits? Yes. Is that bad? No.

Is the Real Problem Change Itself?

Today, the services of lawyers and the legal profession are as important, if not more important, than they have been at any time in American history. Scholars tell us that the greatest challenge of the twenty-first century is dealing with change. Throughout most of human history, the lives of the oldest members of society did not differ substantially from the lives of the youngest members of society. Then, suddenly, all that changed. Fifty years ago, Erik Erikson observed that no civilization in history has ever subjected its members to such rapid and unexpected changes as the United States has.[15] Because lawyers have often been active and effective agents *for* change, there has been a tendency to blame those agents for the effects *of* change—for new ways, about which many of us are unhappy. Yet without the lawyer, society would be ill-equipped to make necessary transitions. The greater the change, the greater the need for law, lawyers, and legal training. And so, over time, Americans have developed a love-hate relationship with the law and with the law's servants.

The Pulitzer Prize–winning lawyer-historian Daniel Boorstin explained in *The Americans: The Democratic Experience* (1973) that it was the lawyer who gave form to the modern age through the expansion of corporations, stock ownership, and trusts.[16] He concluded that those who were law-trained went from deckhands to captains guiding the capitalist ship through the rough, uncharted waters of the industrial age. And these changes helped produce the modern, progressive, and abundant life that is twenty-first-century America.

Lawyers, as value advocates and agents of change, often find themselves under attack at least in part because of changing concepts of morality or new values that clash with traditional ways. Many critics of lawyers are simply critical of the modern age. They condemn lawyers who enforce new laws rather than voters or legislators or regulators who enact the change. For example, the lawyer played by John Garfield in the film *Force of Evil* (1950) is labeled "evil" because of his role in "the numbers racket," a

Myths and Misunderstandings

lottery-like illegal gambling scheme. Over the last quarter of a century, the numbers racket has been replaced by state-approved (and often state-run) lotteries, the proceeds of which are earmarked by the legislature for public education or welfare objectives. Society changes. Indeed, society must change and often does so in unpredictable ways. And it is easy to put the blame on law, lawyers, and judges.

The Abraham Lincolns and Thurgood Marshalls may seize the spotlight of legal history, while the Atticus Finches (*To Kill a Mockingbird,* 1962) and Henry Drummonds (*Inherit the Wind,* 1960) command the silver screen. And yet, every day, thousands of lawyers in law libraries, small courthouses, county welfare headquarters, and public defender offices, unsung as they are, provide equally heroic services. Critics like TV personality Catherine Crier may ask, "Where are the modern-day Atticus Finches and Henry Drummonds?"[17] We say, look around you. They are everywhere. Crier asks, "Where are the enduring myths?" We say that the return of a child stolen from her father, the restoration of fishing rights to a Native American tribe, the reimbursement of fraudulent charges on a struggling student's credit card, the creation of a new and profitable family business, and the closing of a polluting manufacturing plant are all heroic acts. The age of the heroic lawyer has not passed. Look around you! And there are even more heroes currently enrolled or planning to enroll in America's law schools.

If one goes out looking for incompetence and scandal, that is what one is likely to find. Remember the story of the two men who traveled the same stretch of road—one sees gorgeous wildflowers, while the other notices only the rotting wood from which the flowers are growing. You see what you are looking for. We ask Crier, what would be found if a critic with such a negative mind-set went after her heroic Atticus Finch or Henry Drummond? It has been suggested that Finch was outdated in the theories he espoused, that he failed to make defense arguments that were common at the time, and that he conspired with the sheriff to allow Boo Radley to escape charges.[18] Clarence Darrow, on whom the Drummond character is based, was a highly controversial lawyer in his day, rumored to have been involved with jury tampering, bribery, and inciting riots.[19]

We personally agree with Crier that Finch and Drummond are heroic; however, they are no more or less so than the majority of American lawyers who, without fanfare, struggle daily in the pursuit of justice on issues large and small. We need more such lawyers seeking justice. The challenge of this age demands greater, not smaller, numbers of lawyers. Our experience as legal educators suggests that these new lawyers will continue in the historic and heroic mold.

In *The Lessons of History* (1968), Will and Ariel Durant observed that laws may come to differ from earlier moral codes as they adjust themselves to new historical and environmental conditions. Of our present age, the Durants concluded, "The progress of science raised the authority of the test tube over the cross."[20] Thus, we now have a legal system whose primary validator is not a deity, but humankind itself. And this validation is often expressed through humanity's scientific and technological achievements, not its ideals. This shift is at the heart of certain philosophical or spiritual attacks on modern law and lawyers. Scientific achievements, in and of themselves, assert no moral, legal, or ethical ideals or standards of value. These issues are left to be fought out by the lawyers representing often diametrically opposed viewpoints.

American society has chosen law as the primary institution for dealing with these problems, and this decision fuels the nation's need for lawyers. The United States has more than two hundred years of experience in adapting law as an instrument of societal change. "Limited as law is," Justice Felix Frankfurter reminded us, "that's all we have standing between us and the cruelty of unbridled, undisciplined feeling."[21] And it is in our law schools that we prepare the next generation of lawyers to study seriously, in as objective and scholarly a manner as possible, the way to reform law, to make it more responsive to the changing needs of society. Indeed, this is our privilege and challenge as legal educators. In fairness, we must confess that we law professors have not done this as well as we ought. With this book, we hope to join with other legal educators in making legal adaptation to societal change the primary issue for the law school of the twenty-first century.

The coming decades will see major proposals for reforming the way in which the law deals with exploiting new discoveries and new technologies for the greater good, setting high standards for medical and legal professionals, improving the distribution of legal and social services, finding new ways to celebrate and institutionalize human relationships, sharing more equitably the wealth produced by economic growth, ensuring the safety of consumers, and protecting and preserving our natural environment. There is much in law that cries out for reform. We propose—before we rush into new systems—that we carefully weigh the issues of change and risk distribution. Change for the sake of change can be both foolish and costly. Holding to an outdated status quo can be even more tragic.

We propose a study in which legal scholars and students of public policy—including economists and lawyers as well as cultural, religious, business, and medical leaders—evaluate the costs of alternative legal mechanisms. Until such a study is completed, wisdom would suggest a moratorium on major changes in the justice system. The university system, and especially law schools, can be most helpful in such a serious evaluation of public policy. There is also a major role here for the bar, professional disciplinary committees, as well as special interest groups that must be involved in the structuring of such changes.

Determining how to adapt the legal system to changing conditions will not be easy, but the cost of our failure to do so would be monumental. We do not suggest that lawyers alone can guarantee the survival of America's great institutions, but without law and lawyers, the task will be impossible. As one critic of the legal system acknowledged, "Anyone who believes a better day dawns when lawyers are eliminated bears the burden of explaining who will take their place. Who will protect the poor, the injured, the victims of negligence, the victims of racial violence?"[22]

Peter Marshall's parable poignantly demonstrates the great price paid for exiling the keeper of the spring. To dismiss the experience of law and lawyers, to turn our backs on an independent judiciary and the rule of law without a credible and workable replacement, is an option society dare not risk. For more than two centuries, Americans have turned to the law to help society deal with change. Lawyers themselves—and especially legal educators—must be prepared to lead the reforms necessary to bring the legal system into and through the next century.

Lawyers ought not stand aloof from their fellow citizens in addressing the fundamental questions facing the legal system. Lawyers who resist change have the lesson of eighteenth-century Cherokee priests.[23] These traditional lawgivers and medicine men ultimately became the victims of the colonists. This happened, in large part, because they relied on the ways of their precontact law to address postcontact assaults. After the arrival of the

Myths and Misunderstandings

Europeans, a new and different strategy was needed. But the priests could not, or would not, change. It is equally true that present-day law and lawyers must change in order to deal with changed and changing world. New strategies for law and social control are demanded.

As society changes, so does the role of lawyers. More and more lawyers spend their time on issues that rarely existed a hundred years ago, and it looks as if more and more lawyers will be needed in these areas over the next hundred years. A simple example is found in the family and its structure. Hillary Clinton's controversial book, *It Takes a Village* (1996), is a sad reminder that for far too many children, the village or family or clan is not there.[24] In many cases, neither is the father. The grandparents may be the sole caregivers, or they may live too far away to be meaningfully involved.

The domestic relations arena illustrates the truism that lawyers are rarely called, or call, with good news. For every uncontested and happy adoption, there are many more divorces, spousal abuse cases, and child custody battles. Most citizens deal with lawyers only in difficult times. Lawsuits are filed, and court dockets become crowded. Bills are debated by Congress and state legislatures to create new legal structures. These proposals are too often Rube Goldbergesque in design, built by jackleg legislative carpenters to cope with society's changing needs.

It is easy to mistake the symptom for the cause and to blame the lawyers for society's ills. But, like Peter Marshall's keeper of the spring, lawyers are in the business of keeping society working. It is society that gives rise to the problems—not the lawyers. And in an increasingly complex society, these increasingly complex problems give rise to the need for an even greater number of lawyers.

More often than not, lawyers are delivering messages that clients and society do not want to hear—they are, in many cases, professional naysayers. As J. Pierpont Morgan, one of the legal profession's most outspoken critics, proclaimed, "I don't want a lawyer to tell me what I cannot do; I hire him to tell me how to do what I want to do."[25] There is another side to that coin, of course. Elihu Root, the great American lawyer, noted, "About half the practice of a decent lawyer consists of telling would-be clients that they are damned fools and should stop."[26]

How Harmful Are Media-Generated Myths?

As the twenty-first century unfolds and change becomes increasingly rapid, many Americans seem to take pleasure in attacks aimed not only at lawyers and litigators but also at the rule of law itself. The criticism is becoming corrosive. In fact, nothing short of the survival of some of our most basic democratic institutions is at issue. Such attacks on our basic legal structures are fueled by the media through exaggerated or false reporting of actual cases.

The most frequently cited example of lawyer abuse and runaway judgments is the case of Stella Liebeck, the seventy-nine-year-old Albuquerque woman who sued McDonald's after spilling hot coffee and burning herself.[27] The case has been widely reported, but detailed investigations of the facts show just how different the actual case is from the shock newspaper headlines. Among the actual facts of the coffee case, rarely set forth, are the following:

- McDonald's had received more than seven hundred complaints about the temperature of the coffee it

Myths and Misunderstandings

served and had settled many of these, paying out some $500,000.

- McDonald's served its coffee at a temperature twenty degrees hotter than most of its competitors, a temperature at which McDonald's managers admitted that the beverage was too hot to drink right away and hot enough to cause burns.

- Liebeck was hospitalized for a week with third-degree burns requiring skin grafts.

- A jury found in Liebeck's favor, awarding $160,000 to compensate her for her injuries and $2.7 million in punitive damages against McDonald's.

- The jury figured that $2.7 million was the revenue McDonald's took in from two days of coffee sales and used that number as the basis for the punitive damages award.

- The jury found that Liebeck was partially responsible for her injuries and, therefore, reduced the damages it awarded to her.

- The trial judge further reduced the punitive damages award to $480,000, or three times the amount of the actual damages.

- After the verdict and the resulting publicity, McDonald's reduced the temperature of its coffee, and Wendy's reduced the temperature of its hot chocolate, which is often ordered by children.

- Liebeck took two years to recover, and 16 percent of her body was left with permanent scars.

Furthermore, she initially had offered to settle for $10,000 to cover her medical expenses and some compensation for pain and suffering. The trial judge encouraged McDonald's to settle at this figure, but the company refused. McDonald's ultimately settled before an appeal of the jury's verdict was heard and has refused to disclose the amount of the private settlement.

• After surveying temperature samplings from beverages sold at selected McDonald's and other fast food outlets, Carl T. Bogus, of the Roger Williams School of Law, observed that after the Liebeck case, coffee and hot chocolate were much safer. "The McDonald's case may still provide ammunition for tort reforms and late-night talk-show hosts," Bogus concluded, "but it may well have saved many people—children especially—from serious injury."[28]

A detailed examination of other cases raises serious ethical as well as factual questions about how they are represented in the media. Bogus further noted: "There can be little doubt . . . that the misrepresentations are . . . deliberate—at least by those who are furnishing the horror stories, if not by the politicians, journalists and stand-up comedians who are repeating them."[29]

Frequently mentioned among the so-called frivolous lawsuits, runaway judgments, and crazy cases are *Proctor v. Davis* and *Vandevender v. Sheetz*.[30] Under careful analysis, Proctor's claim turns out to be rooted in the failure of a major pharmaceutical manufacturer to report known potential product danger to an eye surgeon; *Vandevender* relates to a valid workers' compensation claim. The exaggerated stories that grew up around these cases—and many,

Myths and Misunderstandings

many others, like them—fail to stand up to careful review, and most of them have been abandoned in serious debate and public discussion. A thorough analysis of these cases shows that they were at the very least misreported, if not deliberately distorted, to create a public image of out-of-control courts and juries. A meticulous review of the records in both cases shows that the decisions were sensationalized and that the truth never caught up with the charges.

Proctor v. Davis gained immediate notoriety when Senator John Danforth, of Missouri, in supporting legislation to curb what he charged was an out-of-control products liability system, told the following story:

> There was a famous case a few years ago of a 70-year-old man who lost the eyesight in his left eye. Now, the loss of eyesight in one eye is not a minor matter. But what is the just result of a 70-year-old man losing eyesight in one eye? What is the reasonable compensation that such an individual should receive? Should it be in the thousands of dollars? In the tens of thousands? The hundreds of thousands? Should it be in the millions of dollars? This person filed a lawsuit, a products liability case, against Upjohn Co., and his recovery was $127 million.[31]

The senator reported nothing else about the case. The story, as he told it, seemed a perfect example of how high verdicts could inhibit pharmaceutical companies from offering new drugs at reasonable prices. This simply is not true.

Meyer Proctor, the plaintiff, was a retired public relations employee in Illinois. He consulted an ophthalmologist named Michael J. Davis for inflammation in one eye. Davis injected a steroid, manufactured by Upjohn, near the eye of the patient. Ophthalmologists had repeatedly asked Upjohn whether the steroid could be administered by periocular injection (injection near the eyeball).

Upjohn never informed the medical community that this use of its steroid product presented potential risks. The company had never conducted appropriate animal or other testing of its product for such use by ophthalmologists. Nevertheless, the company actively encouraged such use of its product. Although the FDA had approved the steroid for other uses, it had never approved the product for periocular injection by ophthalmologists. Davis, on the second administration of the steroid, accidentally inserted the needle into Proctor's eye.

Senator Danforth implied that the $127 million verdict was for the loss of sight in one eye of a seventy-year-old man. Actually, $3,047,819.76 was for compensatory damages to the eye; the lion's share of the award, $124,573,750.00, was for punitive damages—to punish Upjohn for outrageous conduct and deter it and others from similar acts. The trial judge reduced the punitive award to $35 million; after two appellate reviews, the punitive award was further reduced to $6,095,639.52, or roughly two times the compensatory damages. The case was then settled before an appeal to the Illinois Supreme Court. It is instructive to note that Senator Danforth did not ever correct his statement to reflect the actual amount, which was $120 million less than he originally reported. The full facts of the case never caught up with Senator Danforth's sensationalized first account. A fair-minded review shows a thoughtful judicial system checking itself.

Vandevender v. Sheetz has a similar history of factual distortion. The American Tort Reform Foundation posted the following horror story, titled "Pickled Justice," on its Web site:

A West Virginia convenience store worker Cheryl Van-dender [*sic*] was awarded an astonishing $2,699,000 in punitive damages after she injured her back when she opened a pickle jar, according to the *Charleston Daily Mail*. She also received $130,066 in compensation and $170,000 for emotional distress. State Supreme Court Justice Spike Maynard called this award an "outrageous sum," stating in his dissenting opinion: "I know an excessive punitive award when I see one, and I see one here." The court, however, upheld most of the punitive damages: $2.2 million.[32]

The actual facts of the case are quite different. The plaintiff, Cheryl Vandevender, was an assistant manager of a convenience store owned by defendant Sheetz, Inc. She had injured her back and had undergone surgery to correct the problem before taking her job with Sheetz. After about eighteen months on the job, she hurt her back again while opening a large pickle jar, probably aggravating her preexisting condition. After continuing to work for a few months, she began receiving disability payments and subsequently underwent a second back surgery. Several months after the surgery, she informed her manager that she could return to work but could not do any heavy lifting.

The company discharged her, despite a state rehabilitation counselor's contacting the company on her behalf. Contrary to the sensationalized reporting by the American Tort Reform Foundation, she *never* sued about the pickle jar. She instead filed an action against the company for violating the state's workers' compensation law by firing her for a work-related injury and for refusing to rehire her because she had a disability. During the proceedings, the store manager testified that the company's requirement that employees be able to stand for eight hours and lift up to fifty pounds was not actually essential. After giving this testimony, the store manager was fired. The company resisted all attempts by the plaintiff to discover whether the manager had been fired because she had given testimony favorable to the plaintiff.

On the basis of her manager's testimony, the plaintiff asked to return to work. The company agreed to take her back, subject to a medical examination. The examiner cleared her, subject to the limitation of lifting no more than fifteen pounds. When she reported for work, the district store manager feigned ignorance of the medical report and required her to get another medical examination. On doctor's orders, the plaintiff did not return to work.

The action against the company was amended to include a claim that the company's actions when the plaintiff attempted to return to work were in retaliation for her having filed a complaint. A jury awarded the plaintiff $130,066 for lost wages and medical expenses, $170,000 for emotional distress, and $2,699,000 for punitive damages. The trial judge, in refusing to reduce the award, found that the company had a practice of violating the state's workers' compensation laws by firing or refusing to rehire workers. The company conceded that its conduct had been illegal but said that it was due to "mistakes." The judge found the company's claims "simply not credible." In determining whether to reduce the punitive damage award, the judge noted that the company made profits of $1.5 million per day. The Supreme Court of Appeals of West Virginia found that the company's conduct in firing and refusing to rehire fell "into the category of reckless disregard" of the employee's rights. After a careful review of the company's conduct, the court reduced the punitive damage award from $2,699,000 to $2,327,400. Only one judge dissented

Myths and Misunderstandings

on the amount of the punitive damages, and even he agreed that the employee "was treated badly."

In their study "Media Misrepresentations," Laura Beth Nielsen and Aaron Beim compared media representations of lawsuits and the actual litigation to determine whether and why these depictions differ.[33] Nielsen and Beim's representative study was the case of Hiram Clifton, who won a $5.5 million dollar lawsuit for being subjected to racial discrimination.[34] The authors juxtapose the view that such an award for discrimination is a reasonable form of justice with the argument that the plaintiff should have endured the racial gibes. Nielsen and Beim conducted their research by comparing a representative sample of media reports and a random probability sample of actual cases. The research indicated that across the board, the media report judgments for the plaintiff with greater frequency than judgments for the defendant. The data also suggested that employment discrimination cases that end with a victory for the plaintiff are overreported in the media. The media were found to be likely to emphasize large awards yet to downplay the later reversal or reduction of these awards. Lastly, Nielsen and Beim evaluated the potential consequences of the media distortion. They concluded that such misrepresentations shape the public consciousness and that management personnel often rely on such misrepresentations in forming employment policy.

Are Lawsuits the Cause of the Perceived Medical Malpractice Crisis?

Lawyers and courts have been the targets of scathing criticism for causing a medical malpractice crisis. Suing physicians for negligence or medical malpractice is the most frequent example cited of so-called lawyer abuse. Doctors see their medical malpractice premiums skyrocketing. The American Medical Association and powerful insurance company lobbyists inveigh against lawyers and pressure state legislatures, claiming that "outrageously high malpractice verdicts" and "frivolous lawsuits" are the cause.[35] Flat caps on damage awards, no matter how serious the injury or negligent the doctor, are pushed as the cure-all. A detailed review shows these allegations to be vastly overstated and largely false.

Our court system has shown that it has the capacity to weed out frivolous and false claims. When serious injuries or death occur because of bad, reckless, or negligent medical practice, redress through the courts is frequently the victim's only recourse and certainly the fastest. At stake are the rights of patients who have been harmed by doctors. Here are instructive facts about the alleged lawyer-caused malpractice insurance premium crisis.

- The Government Accountability Office (GAO, the research arm of Congress) has reported that this "crisis" of access to medical care as a result of medical malpractice insurance premium increases does not exist or has been overblown.[36]

- The GAO report stated, "The problems [of doctors leaving practice] were limited to scattered, often rural, locations, and in most cases, providers identified long-standing factors in addition to malpractice pressure that affected the availability of service."

- The GAO report was extremely skeptical of the charge that malpractice awards force doctors to engage in expensive and unnecessary defensive medicine. The report noted, among other things, that doctors practice defensive medicine because they make more money by providing those services.

- Medical malpractice payouts, since 1990, have risen more slowly than general medical inflation costs.

- There has been no explosion in malpractice suits against doctors. Data from the National Association of Insurance Commissioners show that from 1995 to 2000, malpractice claims actually declined by 4 percent.[37]

- A key factor in soaring malpractice insurance premium rates was a several-year downturn in the stock market. Insurance company reserves invested in the market did not produce the expected level of profits. To make up for the losses, the companies increased premiums. As a prime example, the St. Paul Companies stopped writing malpractice policies, but the companies' problems came largely from their own investment losses, including at least $70 million in the Enron collapse.[38]

- Medical malpractice is serious. There is, in fact, a substantial national problem arising from day-to-day medical mistakes. The Institute of Medicine reports that between 44,000 and 98,000 hospital patients die every year from preventable mistakes; others suffer permanent and severe injuries.[39]

- The National Practitioner Data Bank reports that only 5 percent of doctors account for the majority of malpractice claims. The medical disciplinary system does not effectively address this issue. Among doctors who have paid more than five malpractice claims, only 12.3 percent have been subjected to disciplinary action.[40]

The most recent data and testimony gathered after the GAO study reinforce the conclusion that there is no lawyer-caused medical crisis. In 2003, for example, Missouri medical malpractice claims fell to an all-time low. In New Jersey, medical malpractice claims declined by 21 percent from 2001 to 2003. In a Florida legislative committee in the summer of 2003, the chief executive of the Florida Medical Association acknowledged, "I don't feel that I have the information to say whether or not there are frivolous lawsuits in the State of Florida."[41] The downward trend continued in 2006 and 2007.

Nonetheless, in recent years, a number of doctors have chosen to surrender what the medical profession had earlier proclaimed as the moral high ground. These doctors have pledged to support a planned refusal to treat. Although scorned by most medical personnel as unprofessional, this movement proposes that doctors refuse to accept as patients either lawyers or the families of lawyers. The South Carolina Medical Association initially endorsed a resolution supporting this tactic. A similar proposal was presented at the 2004 annual meeting of the American Medical Association, but the resolution was withdrawn as "analogous to hitting the lawyer with a 2x4 to get attention." And yet, a number of individual doctors have pledged to refuse to treat lawyers, and others have begun to create a blacklist.[42]

The bitter division within the medical community is highlighted by a proposed hospital and clinic code of conduct focused

Myths and Misunderstandings

on prohibiting medical staff from testifying on behalf of plaintiffs, although the regulations would allow the same personnel to testify as witnesses on behalf of hospitals and doctors. Hysteria and blacklisting reached an extreme in a Longview, Texas, where nurse Selina Leewright was dismissed from her job in a local hospital.[43] Despite her "fantastic nursing skills," she lost her job because her lawyer husband (who did not handle malpractice cases) was a member of a firm that had sued doctors.

We do not intend to imply that all of the bitterness, irrationality, and hostility is on the medical side of the aisle. But the need for better communication and understanding is obvious. Many years ago, Southern Illinois University created a medical-legal program, including a joint JD/MD degree, which the university president hailed as a "peace initiative." "Lawyers and doctors," he noted, "would get to know each other before they met in court."

There is a story, perhaps apocryphal, about a joint appearance at a peacemaking summit between the president of the Texas Medical Association and the Texas Bar Association. As the usual charges, countercharges, horror stories, and refutations were exchanged, the rhetoric of the participants escalated. The doctor accused lawyers of slowing the progress of American medical science. In his closing response, the lawyer shouted: "Medical science! You are witch doctors, not scientists. When lawyers were writing the Constitution, you so-called medical scientists were putting leeches on George Washington's backside." Being from Texas, the lawyer used another more colorful word for that portion of the founding father's anatomy.

In fall 2003, Texas voters narrowly approved a state constitutional amendment capping noneconomic damages on jury verdicts. This cap did not translate into lower malpractice rates for physicians. The Texas Medical Liability Trust reduced its rates by 12 percent, but the next year, the Joint Underwriting Association asked for a 35 percent increase for physicians, surgeons, and other healthcare providers and a 68 percent increase for hospitals. The request was later denied by the Texas Insurance Department.[44]

The Association of Trial Lawyers of America (ATLA), recently renamed the American Association for Justice, has long battled against so-called tort reforms proposed by those who charge, among other things, that the medical malpractice crisis is caused by runaway lawsuits. In responding to public charges by President George W. Bush criticizing the American justice system, the CEO of ATLA, Jon Haber, presented the following statistics to counter the argument about "junk lawsuits" and their effect on the medical community:

> The assertion that fear of lawsuits has reduced the number of individuals choosing medicine as a career is false. According to data from the American Medical Association, the number of physicians is up nearly 90 percent, from 467,679 in 1980 to 884,974 in 2004. In addition, the number of emergency room doctors has gone from 5,699 in 1980 to 27,864 in 2004, an increase of 388 percent. The number of OB-GYNs has increased nearly 60 percent, from 26,305 in 1980 to 42,059 in 2004.[45]

A study of medical malpractice insurers titled *Falling Claims and Rising Premiums in the Medical Malpractice Insurance Industry* has found that insurance companies have been gouging doctors by drastically raising their insurance premiums, even though claims payments have been flat or, in some cases, decreasing.[46] The Justice Department reported that the number of personal injury

Myths and Misunderstandings

cases resolved in the U.S. district courts fell by 79 percent between 1985 and 2003.

After a detailed review of the data from recent medical malpractice developments, *New York Times* columnist Bob Herbert summarized the struggle as follows: "The disinformation campaign of the tort reform zealots, and their sustained attack on the rights of patients who have been harmed by doctors, have been disgraceful. The proper prescription for this apparently chronic disorder is a strong dose of truth."[47]

In the face of the hard data, it seems unnecessary, indeed foolhardy, to cripple our civil justice system by setting artificially low caps on awards to cure a false crisis. One must be either terminally naïve or cynically self-serving to believe that limiting the number of lawyers, the types of litigation, or the size of jury awards will resolve the problems of patients' rights in cases of medical malpractice or other negligent conduct. Society needs to look beyond the surface allegations and into the complexity of modern medicine and the challenge of systematic risk management.

Do These Myths and Misunderstandings Harm Democracy?

Oliver Wendell Holmes Jr. wrote, "Law [is] a magic mirror [in which] we see reflected not only our own lives, but the lives of all men that have been!"[48] Holmes's mirror is a good metaphor. Law is not only central to our society, but it is also the point at which society is ultimately forced to look at itself, to see deeply into the inner workings. Law brings people face to face with change. When things are not working well—when society is out of joint—we see it most vividly in the law. Today, that mirror reflects back to us a particularly disturbing societal image: Not the young and beautiful Snow White we see in our minds' eye, but the aging queen. Breakdowns in society are reflected in the breakdown of the responsiveness of the legal system. And because lawyers are representatives of the legal system, the hostility reflects back on them. It is thus easy to understand why Hitler (as Kenneth Redden reminded us) proclaimed, "I shall not rest until every German sees that it is a shameful thing to be a lawyer."[49]

The legal profession, as the medical malpractice challenge indicates, is crucial in dealing with modern life, with technology, with scientific innovation, and with the shifting values of a new age. It is a cliché of our age that we live in a time of great change, and, like many clichés, it is true—stunningly, irrefutably, absolutely true. In fact, law and lawyers have emerged as the handmaidens of change, often the midwives of change. Virginia's distinguished legal historian Calvin Woodard observed:

> The most cataclysmic phases in the saga of any society, the so-called "water-shed" periods, are those in which fundamental standards are supplanted by new ones . . . . In the last hundred years or so, western societies have gone through, and indeed are still going through, such a cataclysmic phase. We have been in the process of sloughing off an old and adjusting to a new set of standards.[50]

We no longer live in the quiet and gentle world of the cinematic Doctor Gillespie or Judge Hardy, and yet many of us still retain these older, idealized images of the lawyer as a frontier barrister with *Farmer's Almanac* in hand or of the doctor as a house-calling, buggy-driving elder on a Norman Rockwell *Saturday Evening Post* cover. But times change, and both law and lawyers must change to keep up with them.

As a society historically committed to the wisdom of slow evolution of the system of governance, we too often find ourselves dealing through institutions of the horse-and-buggy age while facing the problems of the space age. It is at times like these that the legal profession is put to the greatest test. Lawyers are charged with the reconciliation of the ideal and the actual. Lawyers are expected to help us guide change while ensuring that we remain the same. Lawyers help us sift through the often contradictory evidence and reach a fair and equitable solution, to establish new paradigms rooted in historic structures.

In America, we have historically perceived most problems as having a legal dimension. Indeed, we turn to the courts to ease the pains of change and, upon occasion, as in the integration of public schools, to force change. That keenest of all European observers, Alexis de Tocqueville, noted in *Democracy in America* (1840) that rarely is there a "question in the United States which does not sooner or later turn into a judicial one." With particular reference to the dominance of law, de Tocqueville concluded: "A French lawyer is just a man of learning, but an English or an American one is somewhat like the Egyptian priests, being, as they were, the only interpreter of an occult science. . . . It is at the bar or the bench that the American aristocracy is found."[51] He might have added that it is to the bar and bench that we ultimately turn for solutions to problems that other institutions will not, or cannot, resolve. And to whom do we turn today to blame for unresolved problems? Americans expect lawyers to be medicine men, workers of magic, reconcilers of the irreconcilable— and woe to those who fail to meet expectations.

Judges and justices, too, are subject to attack from all sides of the political spectrum—from the left, from the right, from federalists, from strict constructionists, from implied-purpose interpreters, and from red and blue states alike. The element common to all of this judge-bashing is the lack of a genuine intellectual or factual basis: the chief objection in most, if not all cases, seems to be the failure of the judge's interpretation of the law to comport with the critic's own political bias. Attacks on judges are not new, of course, as the papers of John Marshall, Louis Brandeis, and Earl Warren so clearly demonstrate. Both Earl Warren and William Rehnquist were subjected to "Impeach the Chief Justice" billboards. But in recent years, the bench has become an even more attractive scapegoat. It is as tragic as it is disturbing to see our judges—women and men of good will and keen intellect—subjected to such unwarranted attacks.

Law is, in the final analysis, about values—the way in which a society sees things and decides what it wants done. Today, we lack a clear consensus: our national values are uncertain, often in flux. We are divided—seriously divided. As a people, we Americans do not seem to know who we are or where we want to go. For example, the crisis surrounding the question of abortion as seen in the case of *Roe v. Wade,* is often cast as a question of science—the viability of fetus, as measured in trimesters.[52] And yet, regardless of our own value structure, this is a question of personal choice or rights or bioethics, if not of spiritual ideals or religious faith or moral values.

In many legal issues, such as those relating to the family, old rules and new standards are being worked out in a changed and changing world. It is a world in which critics of both right and left have noted that there appears to have been an end of community. Almost half the children in America are being raised in single-parent households. In the past, close relatives, multi-generational homes, and extended families exerted tremendous social (if not legal) control. For many, these institutions are gone.

At the beginning of World War II, 90 percent of the people in America lived in the county in which they had been born; today, less than 10 percent live in their home county. Americans are said to move, on the average, every three and a half years.[53] A system that depends upon social control rooted in a sense of an actual community—and of a traditional family—will not function in the same way in 2007 as it did in 1907.

And amid these social, economic, and technological changes, some seem to think that there is, or should be, a simple legal or regulatory solution to all problems. Without a doubt, we are a litigious society, but we also have one of the most complex and value-divided civilizations in human experience—and lawyers, judges, and the courts sit in the middle of it. Americans are suing over Little League disputes and attempting to regulate the height of women's platform shoes. Too many of us look for someone else to blame, some other party to pay for what is happening—and that someone is often asked to pay through the result of a lawsuit. And because we look to lawyers and judges to help people solve these problems, we—too often—end up blaming them for the problems that produced the litigation in the first place.

Lawyers are the target and victim of the blame game. The great comedian George Burns, who played the Deity in the film *Oh, God!* (1977), liked to report that "God said 'Let there be Satan, so people don't blame everything on me.'" At which time He added, "And let there be lawyers, so people don't blame everything on Satan."[54]

The increasing number of societal disputes must be seen against the backdrop of higher, greater risks and costs. Our medical and scientific achievements contain both the potential for great advancement and the seeds of potentially monumental mass disaster. Consider a release of poisonous gas in India, a toxic waste spill in Missouri, the danger of asbestos in our elementary schools and our houses of worship, the sad cases of thalidomide babies, and the women made sterile by the Dalkon Shield.

The law to which we look for solutions to these problems is too often the old white hat–black hat law. But if law is to function in this age of rapid change and higher stakes, we must stop thinking of law as a great morality play, as the courtroom entertainment for a hot summer's afternoon, as a shootout between two hired-gun lawyers, as the frontier's legalized battle. Law must become a cooperative venture that seeks to arrive at reasonable ways to distribute unreasonable and unfair risks. Even as we argue that law and lawyers did not cause these problems, law and lawyers are essential to their resolution.

Reform—and the need for reform—is in the air. Nevertheless, we must not forget that sometimes old-fashioned litigation will be inevitable; our historic experience confirms this. Other solutions will also be required if we are to regularize treatment of issues that we as a society would rather not face. Lawyers are addressing new systems and solutions—and legal educators, in particular, must face this challenge daily in our teaching and in our writing. The refusal to face the dangers of the failure of modern technology and the costs of new undertakings is much closer to the root of our current legal crisis than are those whom it is so easy to blame—careless doctors, greedy lawyers, and profit-driven insurance carriers, for example. We are constantly forced to rethink who should bear the risk of conduct—and there is no question that someone, or some institution, must bear these risks. We cannot pretend dangers do not exist, nor can we handle them on an ad hoc basis once they are upon us.

There is a moment in *The Man Who Shot Liberty Valance* (1962) in which Jimmy Stewart, as Ransom Stoddard, a frontier lawyer, argues with John Wayne, as Tom Doniphon, a frontier gunman. In an earlier scene, Lee Marvin, as Liberty Valance, has brutally beaten Stewart and then laughingly torn the pages from his law books. Stewart says to Wayne: "I don't want a gun—I don't want to kill him—I want to put him in jail." Wayne replies: "Oh, [Pilgrim] I know those law books mean a lot to you—but not out here—out here a man settles his own problems." Stewart then collapses from the beating, and Wayne says sarcastically: "Better listen to him . . . He's a lawyer."

As director John Ford tells us with *The Man Who Shot Liberty Valance*—every society changes. And ours has changed and changed mightily over the last century. We have come past the time when John Wayne could address these changes in the street with his gun strapped to his hip, and we have also come past the time when Jimmy Stewart could resolve the crisis of change in a courtroom battle with only his statute book at his side. We must recognize that we are in a new age of social change with new challenges to law and lawyering.

And, of course, there is the matter of perspective. Let us look at a proposed antilawyer resolution "to take some measure to prevent the growing power of attorneys . . . that there may be such laws compiled as may crush or at least put a proper check or . . . restraint on . . . lawyers." As legal educators, we must, of course, be concerned with the impact that this sort of action has on future members of the profession. A Harvard senior considering taking up the study of law verbalized certain doubts about becoming an attorney at "a time when the profession of the law labors under the heavy weight of popular indignation, when it is upbraided as the original cause of all the evils with which the commonwealth is distressed, when the legislature has been publicly exhorted by a popular writer to abolish it entirely, and when the mere title of lawyer is sufficient to deprive a man of the public confidence." And a European textile manufacturer forced to deal with American lawyers put the issue simply: "Is it the multiplicity of law-suits that has engendered the lawyers? Or do not the lawyers give birth to the excess of law-suits?"

These are not new concerns. As you may have guessed, the resolution to prevent the growing power of lawyers by putting a "restraint" on them was passed in 1786 at a town meeting in Braintree, Massachusetts; the Harvard senior was John Quincy Adams as he prepared to enter the study of law in 1787; and the merchant asked his question about the excessive power of lawyers in 1794.[55]

By quoting these historic complaints, we do not want to suggest that our current crisis is not serious or that law and lawyers are not a part of the problem, just as they must be a part of the solution. But a careful review shows that, too often, lawyers and judges are simply convenient scapegoats. We suggest that the tendency to blame the mirror for our wrinkles is not new. Law has always been the point at which societies' breakdowns are most apparent.

We do not expect our book to completely change historic visions and attitudes or even to reduce the number of jokes about the legal profession. We do hope that this review of the myths, together with the presentations of the factual basis behind many of these urban legends, will help keep the role of law and lawyers in perspective. Robert E. Scott, former dean of the University of Virginia School of Law, concluded his discussion of the lawyer as public citizen as follows:

> Popular attitudes toward lawyers will always be contradictory. Popular culture wants to see law as the

overarching principles of a just and harmonious society. Popular morality thus views the lawyer's craft-oriented and client-oriented perspective as an abandonment of every man's duty to justice. But the popular view is simplistic. It fails to recognize the unpleasant reality that our society is not neatly ordered by a universally held and coherent system of values. Ours is a wildly pluralistic culture in which individuals and groups compete to achieve recognition for their private perspectives. As lawyers, we have no answers to these larger social conflicts, rather we strive to speak persuasively for specific sides of these struggles. But, at the end of the day, each of us can take great pride in one bedrock truth: Lawyers are the essential actors in transforming this bubbling social conflict into peaceful change—a change that is fashioned, by lawyers, into institutions that are irritatingly human but also miraculously durable.[56]

LAWYERS ARE
SOCIETY'S PROBLEM SOLVERS

t the most pragmatic level, lawyers are society's professional problem solvers. Lawyers are called upon to make distinctions, to explain how and why cases or experiences are alike or different. Lawyers are expected to restore equilibrium, to be balancers. Every discipline, every profession, every job, and every calling has a cutting edge. At that cutting edge, lines are drawn. Lawyers and judges are society's ultimate line drawers. On one side of the line, the conduct, action, or inaction is proper; on the other side of the line, it is not.

The law establishes the principles that come into play when those critical lines are drawn or crossed—or redrawn, as the case may be. How do we draw those lines? How do we get as close as possible to the line without crossing it? Should the line be moved? Is the line clearly drawn? A typical law school hypothetical, for example, might examine the principles involved in establishing a legal drinking age. Historically, why did some states allow an adolescent who was 18 years and 1 day old to purchase liquor? Why did others forbid one who was 20 years and 364 days old from making such a purchase? Why did yet others distinguish between men and women in setting drinking age requirements?

There is an element unique to the training of lawyers that makes them particularly well-suited for line drawing. In preparing students to become lawyers, a task that begins years before their entry into law school, we seek broad, not narrow, education. Lawyering requires a depth and breadth of knowledge and an understanding of complexities drawn from many disciplines and experiences. Law and lawyering involve much more than learning a set of rules or memorizing the black letter of a body of regulations. Law requires the ability to make subtle distinctions, to draw careful lines. Law schools attempt to shape students' minds to deal with varied challenges and complexities. Therefore, law may be the only graduate discipline in which there are, essentially, no specific undergraduate course requirements. Simply put, in the four years of prelaw undergraduate training, the student's major is not determinative of success in law school or lawyering. Law school admissions officers generally advise prospective students to find the most challenging undergraduate teachers in subjects that truly interest them.

Law schools want their newly admitted students to possess a broad base of undergraduate training, one that shows maturity, high academic achievement, and an ability to excel at difficult intellectual tasks. A student preparing to go to law school may choose to major in almost any discipline—the hard sciences (e.g., biology, chemistry, mathematics, physics), the social sciences (e.g., anthropology, political science, sociology), or the humanities (e.g., history, literature, philosophy)—and still excel in law school. Legal educators have concluded that the specific major does not matter. The heroine of *Legally Blonde* (2001) studied "fashion" and used this knowledge in a dramatic scene of the film to save the accused from the gallows. A student's mastery of a demanding academic program does matter—and matters mightily. But because virtually every college discipline has its own cutting edge in rules and procedures—or line drawing—students from a wide variety of undergraduate backgrounds are qualified for law study. A student with an engineering or mathematics background might end up a patent attorney; a student who majored in psychology might end up a criminal defense attorney. Or they might go on to do something entirely different. But both patent attorney and criminal defense attorney will be molded by a good law school into a professional, a skilled thinker capable of defining a problem and solving it.

Law study challenges a student to respect facts, to identify the legal rule or principle that should be applied, and then to come to a reasoned conclusion as to the outcome. It is what we call "learning to think like a lawyer." Others call it a "nonsurgical lobotomy." Students sometimes describe the experience as a "mental boot camp." Without question, a lawyer's thinking is shaped and reshaped by this educational experience. Students come to understand that every human event—every fact pattern,

Society's Problem Solvers

in the parlance of the legal educator—may be as different as every human fingerprint. Yet the law is a set of rules or principles of general applicability. Law draws the critical line between the proper and the improper, and the facts—the acts of individuals, governments, or corporate entities—fall on one side or the other. As one gets closer to the line, which admits of no straddling, the case becomes harder, and predicting the outcome more difficult. It is the lawyer's job first to get the facts straight, then to identify the legal rules that apply to those facts, and last to give good advice that predicts how a court will apply the relevant rules to that particular set of facts. Sound simple? It is not. It is the legal method, and it requires great skill, reasoning ability, sophistication, and experience. This method is the way in which specific human problems are approached and solved within the legal system. Lawyers are the professionals who are steeped in that system and trained to help resolve problems in a fair and equitable manner, representing the best interests of clients who have varied objectives and values.

As noted earlier, the popular view of the lawyer is as advocate in the courtroom. Resolving legal disputes after a disaster has occurred, is indeed, a classic lawyer role, but we should never forget that the vast majority of potential legal disputes are avoided or solved in advance of litigation by good preventive agreements and defensive lawyering. Well more than 90 percent of actual disputes are resolved before trial through negotiation, mediation, arbitration, plea bargains, and settlement agreements.

Here are a few examples of the many areas of law and the diverse tasks that real lawyers address every day.[1] These are the activities one sees in a real-world lawyer's office, as opposed to the fanciful depictions of television and the movies. We hope these examples provide a window into the life and tasks of America's lawyers.

Wills and Trusts

Everyone dies (despite the best efforts of our medical friends, who may only help us postpone the inevitable), and few of us know when that dread day will come. When we finally get our minds around this distressing fact, we turn to our lawyer. We worry about how to care for our family, how to divide property, how to prevent taxes from consuming our life savings, how to perpetuate our memory through gifts to favorite charities, how to prevent fraud and overreaching, and how to hold down the costs of our burial and administration of our estate.

The lawyer acting as estate planner helps us anticipate those many issues and, through a will (the fancier phrase is "testamentary device" or "trust instrument"), can give us some peace of mind. The estate attorney needs a sophisticated knowledge of property law, probate and gift tax law, intestate succession law (dying without a will), family law, marital property rules, and human psychology. The estate lawyer—like all good lawyers— anticipates the myriad of potential problems and helps solve them before they occur. This is preventive law at its best.[2]

Contracts

Substantial numbers of lawyers work in commercial fields, writing, interpreting, and enforcing business and personal agreements, or contracts. A contract is commonly defined as an agreement between two or more persons, promising to carry out a task, sale, or commitment for mutual benefit. Joe wants to sell his car; Sarah wants to buy the car. A price is agreed on. These terms are all that is required to create an enforceable agreement. But a good lawyer draws a contract that mitigates against future problems.

Society's Problem Solvers

What if the car has hidden defects? What if the money isn't paid on time? What if? What if? What if? Joe and Sarah write an agreement—a contract—and in that agreement, they try to anticipate possible future problems and determine in advance how those problems are to be solved. The legal agreement drafted by the commercial lawyer is not only an instrument of transfer but also a problem-solving agreement. It attempts to anticipate and resolve *future* possible legal problems. Without legally binding contracts, our economy and our commercial world would collapse. The types of contracts—from simple to highly complex— are as varied as the types of arrangements a modern world can conceive. A few of the many kinds of agreements lawyers work with are briefly introduced below:

- Employment contracts. How long is the term? How much is to be paid? What are the benefits? What can be the basis for discharge or layoff?

- Labor agreements. This is also an employment contract, but one that covers many employees; it generally includes a set of terms on minimum compensation, employee discipline, layoffs, strikes, and workplace discrimination, much of which is regulated by labor legislation.

- Sales contracts. The bigger the item, the more the cost, and the more complex the agreement is likely to be. A contract for the sale of a car and a contract for the sale of thirty 747s cover essentially the same set of issues and potential problems. The magnitude of potential legal disputes with the 747s requires a much more sophisticated contract.

- Service agreements. There is incredible variety of agreements under which services, and not goods, are sold. When you contract for custodial services for your ten-story office complex, you have essentially the same issues—but at a more complex level—as when you ask a garage to fix your flat tire.

- Arbitration. Frequently, a contract will anticipate the possibility of legal dispute, and the parties will—in advance—determine that if there is such a dispute, they do not want to engage in a lawsuit. They may name an arbitrator—a private party—as the person or group to whom they will take the problem and agree to follow the arbitrator's decision. This is a form of what is often called "alternative dispute resolution." It is simply another way in which lawyers help individuals plan to solve legal issues before a dispute arises.[3]

Torts

A tort. A wonderful old French word, tort is commonly defined as a personal dispute between private parties arising out of personal injuries, accidents, failed interactions, intentional infliction of emotional and other harm, and defamations. The disputing parties are private—the government usually is not involved. Essentially, the plaintiff (party bringing the complaint) alleges that the defendant is responsible for causing some harm. As redress for that harm, the plaintiff usually seeks monetary damages and, occasionally, an injunction (or order) prohibiting the defendant from continuing similar bad behavior in the future.

Society's Problem Solvers

Torts are as varied as the human condition. Each is defined by a certain number of elements established by statute or by the common law. For a plaintiff to recover on an alleged tort, he or she must prove by a preponderance of the evidence the existence of each element of that tort. In a negligence case, for example, a plaintiff must prove (1) that the defendant's conduct falls below the standard of care that a reasonably prudent person would have exercised in the same or similar circumstances; (2) that the defendant's conduct was the proximate cause of the wrong done to the plaintiff; and (3) that the plaintiff suffered actual harm as a result of this wrong. Medical malpractice, for example, is a tort question.[4]

Crimes

Tort cases are generally between private persons. In a criminal case, the defendant is alleged to have violated a particular law passed to protect the public or the state. The accusing party in a crime is the government, or "the people," as represented by a prosecutor. If a defendant is convicted, the state punishes him or her by fine, imprisonment, or sometimes death.

Like torts, crimes are made up of certain elements, each of which must be proven by the prosecution. At common law, before the advent of comprehensive state penal codes, the crime of robbery was defined as (1) the taking and carrying away (2) of property of another (3) by use of force or fear (4) with the intent to permanently deprive the owner of that property. Note that the definition of a crime almost always involves both a physical element (called the *actus reus*, or guilty act) and a mental element (called the *mens rea*, or guilty mind). Because the stakes are much higher—the defendant's liberty or even life—the standard of proof required is higher as well. The existence of each and every element must by proven by evidence beyond a reasonable doubt.

Historically, the victim of the crime is not compensated; if a criminal defendant is convicted, he or she generally goes to jail. To receive personal compensation for the harm, the victim must bring a separate private tort action against the defendant. Criminal law is designed to keep public order and protect citizens. Tort law compensates private victims. Some torts arise out of the same fact patterns as crimes but must be litigated separately. For example, if one causes a traffic accident while driving under the influence of alcohol, the state will bring a criminal case to punish the violation of the law enacted to preserve public safety. But an individual victim who suffers property damage or personal injuries in that accident must file a tort claim to seek compensation for those losses.[5]

Military Law

A separate system of rules and procedures, called the Uniform Code of Military Justice, governs military issues and members of the armed forces. Society has determined that order and strict discipline are so essential to the military, particularly in time of armed conflict, that a separate body of law is needed. Military lawyers (judge advocates) both prosecute and defend officers and enlisted personnel charged with violations of military law. There are often interesting points of conflict between military and civilian courts.[6]

Administrative Tribunals

Administrative agencies created by acts of Congress or state legislatures may be empowered to promulgate and enforce a wide variety of specialized rules and regulations. Increasingly large numbers of regulatory and economic issues come before administrative law judges, hearing officers, or other magistrates working within these agencies. For example, the Internal Revenue Service has the power to promulgate rules governing tax collections, and the agency can hold hearings in which private lawyers and lawyers for the government appear. These rules are designed to both preserve the government's rights to collect the revenue necessary to run the government and the taxpayer's individual rights to be taxed only for legitimate purposes.[7]

Family Law

Often special courts and rules exist to handle family or children's issues, juvenile crimes, divorce, and custody decisions. These are among the most vexing of all areas. Because of the importance of the issues involved—the most basic and fundamental human relationships—lawyers must represent the interests of all parties. For example, each spouse in a divorce and custody proceeding will usually retain counsel, but the court may also appoint a guardian ad litem (often a lawyer or other law-trained individual) to represent the best interests of the minor children in the case.[8]

Every day, in courtrooms throughout the land, lawyers work to protect the individual rights of litigants and to preserve public order. Lawyers, as earlier suggested, are the foot soldiers of the Constitution—the guardians of basic, fundamental rights. They are the keepers of the springs who prevent the streams of democracy from becoming clogged or dammed. The right to worship or not worship as one sees fit, the right to be free of state-imposed religious strictures, the right to speak freely, the right to publish without censorship, the right to protest peacefully—all of these and many other rights are essential to the day-to-day operation of our free society.[9] If charged with a crime, every citizen is entitled to be represented by counsel, to have a fair and impartial judge and jury, to cross-examine witnesses against him, to stand silent, and to require the state to prove every element of the crime beyond a reasonable doubt—and, all the while, to be presumed innocent until proven guilty.

Democracy can be a messy business. It is natural for human beings to desire unfettered freedom to express personal views but at the same time to harbor a desire to control or censor the opinions of others whom they regard as ignorant or just unorthodox. True tolerance, respect for diversity in all its forms, and the free flow of public discourse are at the core of American values. There is no task more fundamental than the preservation of the protections contained in our Bill of Rights. Each of us is an individual entitled to respect for our own human dignity. Even the most dislikable or seemingly evil member of the polity is still entitled to these protections.

Lawyers serve individuals and society in a wide variety of ways. We must not forget that lawyers, in addition to being the guardians of fundamental rights, are also the architects and carpenters who build and repair our commercial world, who keep the wheels of commerce turning. Lawyers represent individuals and businesses as both outside and in-house counsel. Lawyers both advocate for change and argue for the status quo by representing interest groups in all varieties of public policies. Lawyers serve on town councils, in city halls, in state legislatures, and in Congress. Lawyers fight to protect against unfair advantage, overreaching, or overregulation. Lawyers represent citizens' groups seeking zoning changes or environmental protection; they also represent private landowners seeking protection from confiscatory government policies. Welfare and poverty laws, access to public health, issues of educational opportunity—like the great affirmative action debates—can be hot controversies in which lawyers often stand front and center. Vibrant public debate, most often conducted or directed by lawyers, refines our policy making and initiates reforms in the legal system itself.

Legal issues often involve strong feelings. Although most clients respect their own personal lawyer, the lawyer on the other side, representing the opposing view, is often a target of scathing criticism. But that is the nature of the democratic beast. From the town hall to the Congress and through all three branches of government, from the union hall to the corporate boardroom, from the cleaning of our air and water to the testing of our fruits and vegetables, from the proper administration of public resources to the protection from arbitrary powers—in the library, on the Internet, at regulatory sessions, and in the courtrooms—in all walks of life, lawyers are at the cutting edge. Where the parts grind together, you will find the lawyer.

Inevitably, as the number of business transactions increases, many individuals do try to take advantage of each other, particularly in the economic realm. For example, one laundry owner, whose business flourishes in a free-enterprise society, may decide to solidify his position by squeezing out another local laundry woman, the new competitor in town. He can then monopolize the laundry business and raise prices. This small case is an example of a larger societal issue. Society, in turn, may choose to respond to such action with economic regulations, such as antitrust laws designed to discourage predatory practices and to preserve free markets.

- At the end of the nineteenth century and the beginning of the twentieth, large companies monopolized whole industries. So-called trust-busters crafted sections 1 and 2 of the Sherman Act, the core of our antitrust protections.[10] It is a story of great change—one in which lawyers helped argue, draft, enact, administer, and enforce legislation protecting free markets and fair competitive practices. It is the story of reform, of the free-enterprise system purging itself through law, not revolution.

- One of the first great antitrust actions under the Sherman Act was the *American Tobacco* case.[11] That corporate giant controlled more than 90 percent of all tobacco sales. The U.S. Supreme Court ordered American Tobacco to divest, creating three smaller companies; James B. Duke, the powerful tobacco baron, had to sell two-thirds of his holdings. The resulting cash fortune—and perhaps a guilty conscience and a good estate lawyer—enabled him to establish the Duke endowment, creating a great university where Trinity, a small Methodist college, once stood. And Duke Power Company electrified large sections of the Southeast. Free markets were created where monopoly had existed, and great charitable enterprises were founded with the proceeds from the divested stock. The law was used as a tool to preserve and protect freedom of enterprise. Our capitalist system thus flourished; the streams of commerce freely flowed.

- The fight to preserve free enterprise echoed throughout the last century and reverberates even more vigorously today. The stock market collapse

Society's Problem Solvers

in 1929 resulted in what became known as an
alphabet soup of new agencies created to combat
effects of the Great Depression. More recently, the
controversial film *Erin Brockovich* (2000) depicted
the need for continued citizen protection from
concentrated economic power; the Enron disaster
resulted in the Sarbanes-Oxley Act to protect
investors from fraudulent accounting practices;[12]
and after Martha Stewart's imprisonment, investors
may be more wary of using insider tips.

The complexity of our economy and the need to protect the public, on the one hand, and the competing need to avoid economic overregulation, on the other, make lawyers essential. Nonetheless, lawyers frequently come under attack precisely because they represent all sides of these great economic questions.

Deep in the origin of law is the need of society to regulate itself—not just relations among the members of the tribe or band or family or clan but also its relations with other tribes and bands and families and clans. One sees this most basic need in the rule of law described in the Old Testament: "Ye shall have one manner of law, as well for the stranger, as for one of your own country."[13] This view has been clear through much of human history but seems even more essential in the global economy of the twenty-first century. "Justice," the great nineteenth-century lawyer Daniel Webster argued, "is the ligament which holds civilized beings and civilized nations together."[14]

THE AMERICAN LEGAL SYSTEM HAS BUILT-IN SAFEGUARDS TO ASSURE FAIRNESS AND TO PROTECT CITIZENS' RIGHTS

Courts, judges, and lawyers play a vital and historic role in American civilization. To keep our democracy vibrant, citizens must feel they have a fair forum in which to settle grievances. The bases for final decisions must be open and transparent. Justice must be equal for all, and it must be accessible to all. We are still a very long way from perfection. Over the last century, however, we have made enormous strides. Nonetheless, some of the devices used by American lawyers to open access to the courts are the objects of attack. These instruments, some examples of which are outlined below, are crucial to ensuring that the courts are not just for the wealthy or privileged.

Critics of lawyers too often illustrate the old adage about executing the messenger—condemning the bearer of bad news. And there is no doubt that lawyers must often be the bearers of news we do not want to hear. Lawyers remind us of problems we do not wish to face. It is important to remember, however, that for all their importance to the functioning of our legal system, lawyers are *not* the force that drives it. When a lawyer files an action, it is at the behest of a client—an individual, a business, or a government entity—that has decided to take steps to address some problem—a personal injury, a breached contract, or a code violation. And when cases are tried, it is the juries and judges—not the lawyers—who make the decisions.

The fact that a lawyer files a suit does not mean automatic liability for the defendant or automatic recovery for the plaintiff. To illustrate this point, new law students are often introduced to a wonderful old legal adage "You can sue the bishop of Boston for bastardy, but that doesn't necessarily mean you can recover." Citizens are, of course, entitled to their day in court, and to automatically preclude some person or group from bringing a claim, just because some other person or group might view the claim as frivolous—or simply against its own interests—would stifle access to justice.

It is often the filing of a suit, not the resulting decision, that is the basis for news stories and subsequent attacks on the legal profession—the dismissal of a highly controversial lawsuit often goes unreported in the press. For example, there was worldwide publicity when a group of obese people sued a number of fast-food chains, claiming that they should have been warned of the health risks of overindulging in the chains' products. An avalanche of criticism of lawyers and of our legal system followed the reports of the filing of these claims. A few weeks later, the suit was dismissed on a motion for summary judgment. The dismissal received scant media attention.[1] The point is not that a questionable grievance was filed, but that a well-established legal system exists to dispose of suits that, upon more careful investigation, turn out to be without merit. A simple motion was filed in response to the initial suit; basically, the motion said that the allegations were without merit and that there was no legal cause of action or basis for recovery. A judge considered the matter and ended the case before trial, thus stopping the expenditure of time and money on a meaningless pursuit. The legal system checked itself against abuse, while providing a channel for the review of the complaint. Critics may clamor about the absurdity of the initial charges in the lawsuit, but in this instance, as in thousands of others each year, the system worked.

Just as the myth may endure far longer than the short-lived lawsuit on which it was based, so may the results of the accompanying media frenzy. After the case had quietly disappeared, the Wisconsin legislature passed an act to prohibit similar suits against fast-food operators. Having determined there had never been such a suit in the history of the state, Governor Jim Doyle vetoed the bill.[2] Such overreactions to potential lawsuits are the result of what law school professors often call "imaginary horribles." A dozen state legislatures enacted "cheeseburger laws" designed to protect the fast food industry.[3]

Safeguards against Frivolous Civil Suits

The dismissal of a claim is just one of the many ways in which the legal system winnows the wheat from the chaff before allowing the parties in a civil case to engage in an expensive and time-consuming trial.[4] Other pretrial safeguards include the motion for judgment on the pleadings, which asks the judge to decide the case on the basis of the plaintiff's complaint and the defendant's answer;[5] the motion for summary judgment, which is similar to the motion for judgment on the pleadings but alleges specifically that there is no genuine issue of material fact for the jury to hear;[6] and the motion for judgment as a matter of law—also known as a directed verdict—which alleges that a party has failed to make out a case and that no reasonable jury could find in that party's favor.[7] Each of these simple rules provides another exit point for frivolous, unfounded, or simply weak cases.

Furthermore, whenever an attorney files papers on behalf of a client, he or she must certify to the court that the filing is not being made for an improper purpose; that the legal contentions are warranted by existing law or by a nonfrivolous argument for a change in that law; and that all statements or denials have evidentiary support. If the court later determines that the attorney has violated any of these obligations, it may impose sanctions on the attorney or the law firm.[8] In addition to these in-court proceedings, the attorney also faces the possibility of disciplinary action—even disbarment—for violations of ethical rules relating to the filing of frivolous lawsuits.[9] The prospect of financial penalties or the loss of livelihood should make the prudent attorney think long and hard about bringing an action unsupported by the facts.

The pretrial period also provides time for the parties to work through their differences privately, through negotiation and settlement. Parties are free—indeed, are positively encouraged—to engage in good-faith efforts to resolve issues outside of court. Here again, the services of the lawyer can be key to a successful outcome: the lawyer as negotiator, either before or after the filing of a suit, may be able to avoid the need for protracted litigation. The emergence of the alternative dispute resolution (ADR) movement is a superb example of systemic self-correction and self-improvement. It provides another voluntary way for parties to resolve their differences peacefully, by agreement and without litigation.

Roles of the Judge and Jury

When a real grievance exists, and there is no way to avoid a courtroom confrontation, our trial process is the envy of the world. An independent judge acts as the presiding officer. Each side has the right to be represented by a lawyer whose ethics require zealous protection of the client's interest. Trials are transparent and open to the scrutiny of press and public. Evidence is introduced in open court, and witnesses are subject to cross-examination. An independent jury of laypeople acts as the fact finder, proceeding under rules set out by the judge.

Overall, we have very good reason to trust juries. Our long historic experience with the jury system confirms its wisdom and fairness. Jurors are not jaded by sitting on an endless stream of similar cases; they are the peers of the litigants; and they swear that they will try to arrive at a fair result in that particular case. We trust our fellow citizens to bring their good common sense to the solutions of serious problems. Of course, juries can and do make mistakes. When this happens in a civil case, a party may file a motion for a judgment notwithstanding the verdict; if convinced that the jury made an error, the judge can set aside the verdict and order a new trial. Judges, as well, can and do make mistakes, and these mistakes of law can be taken on appeal to a higher court for review.

Built-In Safeguards

Role of the Expert Witness

As noted above, lawyers do not decide the outcome of cases. Juries decide cases. Juries are drawn from the population at large, and this can be both an advantage and a disadvantage. The jurors' disinterest in the outcome of a case, their varied backgrounds and experiences, and their good common sense combine to make the jury an excellent fact finder. But legal disputes often arise over highly complex technical issues, particularly in civil cases: Does a blow to the head (blunt trauma) cause glaucoma? Does the taking of the drug Bendectin by a pregnant woman cause birth defects?

Our court system helps the jury decide such complex questions by allowing lawyers to call expert witnesses—persons who by education, training, or skill have capacity in areas that are beyond the knowledge of the average lay juror. The expert witness is a powerful tool to aid the jury in its search for the truth, and, like any tool, it may be subject to misuse in the hands of the unscrupulous. But even if it were true, as some critics have alleged, that trials have become nothing more than swearing contests between highly paid and highly partisan experts, the fault lies not in the tool but in the user. Large corporate enterprises, as developers of new commercial products, have been particularly critical, charging that plaintiffs often call experts whose raison d'être is to assert that the corporation's product is the cause of the plaintiff's condition. These critics allege that such experts rely on "junk science"—or unproven theories—to support the plaintiffs' claims and assert that the fear of large verdicts can cause a business to withdraw or withhold useful products from the marketplace.

But the courts' treatment of expert testimony is another example of how the American judicial process contains within itself the mechanisms required to check the excesses of any of its constituent parts. The standard set by the U.S. Supreme Court in *Daubert v. Merrell Dow Pharmaceuticals* requires trial judges to evaluate proffered expert testimony that purports to rely on science and to determine whether the testimony is, in fact, based on *real* science.[10] Before the jury is allowed to hear the expert's testimony, the trial judge must determine both that the evidence is relevant to the issue at hand and that it is reliable—that is, whether the theory or technique in question has been subject to extensive testing, whether it has undergone peer review by other scientists in the same field, whether it has known error rates or established standards, and whether there is a general level of acceptance within the relevant scientific community. Furthermore, courts may call to the stand their own neutral experts, not sponsored by either party, following the European or civil law practice.

The Contingent Fee, Court Costs, and Attorney Fees

Although the courts are open to all, professional legal representation is a service that must be paid for. (The one general exception is the defense of indigent persons accused of a crime, as outlined below.) The legal system, therefore, has developed tools to enable less-affluent plaintiffs to bring suit for redress of their legitimate grievances as well as to protect defendants from the potentially ruinous costs of their vindication.

Our society has chosen to provide access to courts for those who have been injured, defamed, or defrauded through the contingent fee: the client does not pay the lawyer a fee unless a settlement or recovery is actually made. In exchange for undertaking representation of the client without an up-front payment—or guarantee of any payment at all—the lawyer typically receives an agreed-upon percentage of the settlement or verdict. If the lawyer wins a large verdict for her client, the lawyer reaps a proportionally large reward for her services. Unquestionably, the contingent fee can be abused, and for that reason there are certain restrictions on its use. The contingent fee is not available, for example, in actions for divorce or in the defense of persons accused of a crime. It is worthy of note that in just such cases, alternative sources of funding for representation of indigent clients are frequently made available by legislative act. The contingent fee plays an important role in leveling the playing field between injured and impoverished plaintiffs and wealthy tort-feasors.[11]

Sometimes, however, the defendant is the little guy. A large corporation, for example, may target a vocal critic of its environmental or labor practices with a suit for defamation, although the critic's statements may be matters of opinion (and therefore not defamatory) or may be entirely factually true and accurate. The object of the suit is not to protect the good name of the corporate client: it is to force the defendant to shut up and go away. The cost of defending oneself against such strategic lawsuits against public participation (SLAPP suits) can run into the tens of thousands of dollars, beyond the means of even relatively financially secure individuals.

In such situations, the victorious defendant may file a motion for the award of costs and attorney fees—in other words, a request that the court order the plaintiff to pick up the bill for dragging the defendant into court. The decision usually lies in the discretion of the court, but some statutes contain provisions to award costs and attorney fees to the prevailing party.[12]

Punitive Damages

Punitive damages (or judgments assessed to punish bad behavior) draw attention to abusive practices and force defendants—

who might otherwise ignore injuries, or even deaths, as an acceptable cost of doing business—to address bad policies, shoddy products, or dangerous practices.[13] For example, the deceptive practices of tobacco companies and the danger of their products were exposed after lengthy litigation that resulted in substantial punitive damage awards. The size of these awards caught the attention of corporations and their officers. Pushing cigarette sales to teenagers with grossly misleading, but attractive, advertising is no longer tolerated. Firestone Tire and Ford Motor Company could no longer point fingers at each other while continuing to ignore dangerous products in the face of the threat of high punitive damage awards. There will always be a tug-of-war about punitive damages, over how much is fair or how much is needed as a deterrent. But even when the jury has been persuaded to award punitive damages many times greater than the actual damages suffered by the plaintiff (as in the *Liebeck v. McDonald's* and *Proctor v. Davis* cases discussed in chapter 2), the system contains a built-in check against such excesses. The judge has the power to review the award and to adjust it downward to meet the dictates of justice: high enough for the defendant to feel the sting, but not so high as to bankrupt an entire industry.

Constitutional Protections for Those Accused of a Crime

In every criminal case, the state is bringing its weight to bear on the individual charged. The power of the government is immense; the individual often stands alone. For this reason, the presence of the lawyer is crucial in criminal cases. Our system places great value on the intrinsic dignity of the individual and therefore provides the accused with a presumption of innocence until the state bears its burden of proof, beyond a reasonable doubt, on every element of the crime charged. Yet we have critics who take arrest of an accused as sufficient evidence, standing alone, for a guilty verdict, who see a failure of justice when the accused is not convicted. Attacks on judges often grow out of criminal cases in which a law enforcement officer or prosecutor thinks he has produced adequate evidence to arrest or hold a suspect, but the judge disagrees about its value. Or the evidence, although sufficient, may have been improperly procured—for example, in violation of constitutional limitations on searches and seizures or through the use of coercive methods to extract a confession—forcing the judge to exclude it from court proceedings. Often condemned as let-'em-loose justice by critics of America's criminal law, these basic rights are absolutely essential. They include the following:

- An accused has the right to a lawyer and must be informed of that right.

- An accused has the right of silence.

- An accused cannot be compelled to testify, and only the accused, exercising free choice, can decide whether to take the stand. The prosecutor cannot comment if an accused decides to remain silent, and the judge must instruct the jury not to consider an accused's silence against him.

- An accused can have his lawyer cross-examine all witnesses against him.

- An accused may challenge his detention by writ of habeas corpus, compelling the state authority to provide a reason for the deprivation of liberty.

- An accused may file motions to exclude illegally
  obtained evidence, such as coerced confessions or
  physical evidence seized from his home or office
  without a valid warrant issued upon a judicial
  finding of probable cause.[14]

These basic rights remain the bulwark of a free society. Unquestionably, they make it harder to convict the accused—and that is a good thing, not a bad thing! These constraints force the police to do their jobs with diligence and not to rely on sloppy proof or gut instinct. They are evidence not of laxity or softness but of the rigorous discipline that the founders of this nation built into the criminal legal system. Lawyers exist to see that these rights are enforced, that discipline is maintained. Those who would benefit by easier convictions or whose philosophy does not admit of a presumption of innocence form one group of vocal critics of defense lawyers and judges. Others simply disagree with the outcome of a particular case. And much of what passes for media reporting on controversial trials focuses on the self-serving claims of such interested parties. But much more is at stake than the feelings of the criminal defense bar or the conviction rate of prosecutors.

A mistake in a criminal trial is extremely serious. The conviction of an innocent person not only is a personal tragedy but leaves the real criminal at large in society. On the other hand, if a guilty person goes free, society is not protected from an individual who may commit another crime. The American legal system strikes the balance on the side of protecting the individual defendant. It presumes innocence until there is proof of guilt beyond a reasonable doubt. An acquittal by a jury is usually the end of the matter; the constitutional safeguard against double jeopardy prevents the accused from being tried twice for the same offense. If the jury brings a verdict against the accused, the courts of appeals are open to hear his plea for vindication.

Self-Policing Efforts of the Legal Profession

No profession is perfect, and the legal profession is no exception. Just as there are good doctors and bad doctors, good journalists and bad journalists, there are also good lawyers and bad lawyers. Today many lawyers, judges, and legal educators are focused on improving both the quality and fairness of legal services in a number of areas.

The legal profession has a strong and vigorously enforced ethical code. The Model Rules of Professional Conduct establish high standards for lawyers. The bar disciplinary process is active and responsive. Lawyers openly criticize the conduct of their fellow practitioners. The legal profession's dirty linen is often washed in public. The bar is not a closed guild whose primary function is to protect its members. Lawyers fight over misconduct publicly, and serious disciplinary actions (including disbarment) are regularly carried out. The American Bar Association, the Commissioners on Uniform State Laws, the American Law Institute, and legal educators regularly evaluate and encourage higher ethical standards. Nonetheless, still more aggressive self-disciplinary action would do much to strengthen confidence in the profession.

The ABA president, judges, practicing lawyers, law professors, and bar officials meet regularly to address all sorts of professional concerns, such as affirmative action, pro bono service, and the need for active continuing legal education. The ABA's Standing Committee on the Federal Judiciary reviews and critically comments on the strength of nominees to the federal bench. The ABA's Section of Legal Education and Admissions to the Bar is the Department of Education's recognized accrediting agency for law schools. The improvement in accreditation standards over the last half century has resulted in dramatic advancement in the quality of the educational experience at approved law schools. The ABA's *MacCrate Report*, which focused on the need for more practical legal skills training, has helped transform law school curricula. The Association of American Law Schools conducts workshops, scholarly sessions, and conferences; it also publishes the quarterly *Journal of Legal Education,* which contains serious academic studies suggesting ways to improve legal education and the profession. Virtually every law school begins orientation with a strong dose of professionalism and ethical vision and continues this through graduation. The Law School Admission Council is dedicated to finding ways to increase the fairness of the selection process for new law students and to expanding diversity within the profession.[15]

Every year, thousands of continuing legal education courses are offered to lawyers to keep them up-to-date and to improve their knowledge and performance. Most states require lawyers to attend continuing legal education in order to retain their license to practice. Furthermore, virtually all state bars require a specific number of hours of legal ethics or professionalism training. Bar conferences on legal reform issues and special workshops are frequently held and affect not only the members of the profession but also state and federal policies.[16]

The profession has also worked hard to inculcate in its practitioners the habit of service to the less fortunate. Legal aid programs, law school clinics, and prepaid legal services reflect the profession's efforts to broaden the accessibility of legal services.

Built-In Safeguards

For example, at our home institutions—the University of Oregon and South Texas College of Law—special clinics have been funded to provide legal help to individuals seeking refuge in local programs for battered spouses. Many other law schools, led by Southern Methodist University and Tulane University, require pro bono service of each student before he or she can graduate. Every law school and virtually all state and county bars have pro bono initiatives that provide free legal services for the public good. In 2006, law students at the University of Oregon served the community with more than eleven thousand hours of pro bono work. The lawyer's ethical code creates a duty to perform such service. Few other professions, if any, provide so much free service and with almost no public recognition or credit.[17]

"During the past decade," former ABA president Dennis Archer reports, "the [Bar] Association has initiated more than 600 programs addressing a wide range of public concerns—from child abuse to the legal problems of the elderly, from the rights of alleged terrorists to protection of military dependents, from domestic violence to professional responsibility of lawyers, from juvenile crime to issues facing the homeless."[18] The work of the American Bar Association, the Fund for Justice and Education, and the American Bar Endowment "continues to make a substantial difference not just in providing expanded and improved legal services and opportunities, but also in responding to important issues facing the country."

Reform: Who Needs It and Why

Despite all the checks and balances outlined above, despite the discipline enforced from within and from without, there are serious problems in our legal system, especially in delivery of legal services. In attempting reform, the list of issues that the profession must address is long:

- Formal litigation costs too much and takes too long, and its procedures are frequently too complex.

- Legal services should be available to all segments of society.

- Preventive legal services should be available to reduce the number of costly disputes.

- More systems of alternative dispute resolution are needed.

- Citizens need better information about our democracy and how law works; legal education for the general public is crucial.

- Secondary and undergraduate courses in basic legal issues should be more readily available, if not required.

- The legal profession must be more vigorous in its policing and disciplining of lawyers who violate the professional standards and values.

- The legal profession needs more diversity; it is indisputable that the viewpoints of minority groups, the elderly, women, and the poor will be better heard if more members of these groups become lawyers.[19]

No, the legal profession, and the lawyers and judges who work within it, are not perfect. But improvement is substantial and on-going. Lawyers and the legal profession are dedicated to creating positive change, and few, if any, professions more publicly examine and acknowledge shortcomings or work harder to clean house.

LAWYERS HELP CREATE
A MORE JUST SOCIETY

there is no better example of lawyering in the public interest than the twentieth-century American civil rights movement, and one of America's most compelling civil rights sagas is the struggle for equal educational opportunity. Most informed Americans know that more than fifty years ago, the U.S. Supreme Court's decision in *Brown v. Board of Education* declared that segregation of public school children solely on the basis of race violated the equal protection clause of the Fourteenth Amendment.[1] But how that case was brought by a small band of lawyers, led by the NAACP and Thurgood

Marshall, is a dramatic story of faith and dedication as well as consummate lawyering skill and pure courage. After *Brown* was decided, that story had barely begun.[2]

The *Brown* decision was not self-executing. In the implementation decision, *Brown II*, the Supreme Court ordered desegregation of the public schools to begin.[3] Concerned about resistance and foot-dragging in the Deep South and border states, the Court directed that enforcement was to proceed "with all deliberate speed." Thus began a social and legal revolution that lasted thirty years, one whose echoes still reverberate.

For the first ten years, there was, at best, tokenism. Protracted litigation in New Orleans, for example, resulted in the enrollment of only four black children in a previously all-white school—and then the school was boycotted by angry whites. Two federal judges in New Orleans, J. Skelly Wright and Herbert Christenberry, faced death threats and had to be guarded around the clock by federal marshals. Meanwhile, President Dwight D. Eisenhower federalized the Arkansas National Guard to integrate Little Rock Central High School, and the 82nd Airborne Division occupied Oxford, Mississippi, for a year to integrate Ole Miss. This was only the tip of the iceberg of resistance. While Congress stood on the sidelines, courageous federal trial judges and appellate judges issued thousands of integration orders throughout the country. Those orders were the result of claims filed on behalf of individual children by a band of determined lawyers.[4]

In the center of the maelstrom, appellate judges like Elbert Tuttle, John Minor Wisdom, Richard Rives, and John R. Brown of the U.S. Court of Appeals for the Fifth Circuit held the line set down by the U.S. Supreme Court. Threatened, beleaguered, and sometimes ostracized, federal trial judges, like Frank Minis Johnson in Alabama and Gerald Tjoflat in Florida, did not flinch. Racial desegregation ultimately came in the 1960s and 1970s, transforming the legal landscape of the nation. Constitutional promises were kept. It was the lawyers and judges who made the law live—and in so doing, bettered the daily lives of millions of children. Their actions translated a controversial Supreme Court decision into the law of the land. The rule of law, not the threat of mob action, prevailed. Although the desegregation battle is, for the most part, won, related issues like affirmative action will continue to be litigated well into the twenty-first century.

A 2007 U.S. Supreme Court case signals that the great desegregation battles that began in *Brown I* and *Brown II* have not ended. Poverty and entrenched housing patterns have effectively resegregated many previously integrated public schools. On June 28, 2007, the Supreme Court found that school districting programs implemented by Seattle, Washington, and Louisville, Kentucky—which took race into account for the express purpose of preserving integrated schools—violated the equal protection clause of the Fourteenth Amendment.[5] Critics question whether this signals an erosion of the promises of equal education opportunity made by *Brown*. They ask how school boards can preserve long-fought-for gains in achieving integration without taking race into account. Some go even further and claim that *Brown I* is being turned on its ear. These new Supreme Court cases do, in fact, indicate that the battles to achieve racial equality are far from over.

An equally apt illustration of the rule of law in the struggle for basic human rights is the courts' interpretation of historic treaty language in a series of Indian fishing cases, which culminated in *United States v. Washington*.[6] This is a stirring example of the role that lawyers and judges play in the peaceful resolution of deep conflict. Native peoples of the Pacific Northwest lived—both physically and spiritually—on the harvest of salmon and other fish from the great rivers and oceans that surrounded their homelands. Beginning in the 1850s, the Indians entered into a series of treaties, under which they agreed to surrender large portions of their aboriginal lands but reserved the right to continue to fish "at the usual accustomed places" and to harvest fish "in common" with the white treaty signers.

By the 1960s and 1970s, the Native treaty signatories were getting only a miniscule portion of the fish caught in these waters. There came together an informal coalition of militant tribal fishermen such as Billy Franks, brilliant legal scholars such as Ralph Johnson, dedicated lawyers such as David Getches, and farsighted public interest law firms such as the Native American Rights Fund (NARF). The question of Native fishing rights was soon before the courts in Oregon and Washington, and it eventually reached the U.S. Supreme Court. The resulting decisions, which upheld the Indians' interpretation of the treaty language— that is, that the "in common" provision entitled the tribes to 50 percent of the total allowable catch—led not only to the revitalization of the Native fishing harvest and its accompanying cultural rebirth but also to improved conservation and commercial fishing opportunities for all. Similar litigation arose with regard to the fishing rights of indigenous peoples of the Great Lakes area, where there was ultimately a resolution favorable to the Indian nations.[7]

For forty years, the tobacco industry had won every case brought against it—that was, until Richard Scruggs appeared. Richard Scruggs is a small-town plaintiff's attorney from Mississippi, who started his career with class action lawsuits against the asbestos industry. Scruggs used his own money, more than

$9 million from his successes in the asbestos cases, to tackle Big Tobacco in a Mississippi courtroom. In 1997, Scruggs and Mississippi's attorney general, Michael Moore, sued thirteen tobacco companies on behalf of the state's taxpayers in order to recover money expended on health care for smokers.[8]

The two lawyers traveled across the country, eventually convincing the attorneys general of some forty other states to join their cause. In addition, Scruggs and Moore protected two very important whistleblowers, including the first high-level tobacco executive to turn against the companies. Once the tobacco industry was forced to the negotiating table, the companies agreed to pay an astonishing $368 billion in health-related damages. Among the achievements of the settlement were a $25 billion trust for tobacco-related medical research, a ban on all outdoor advertising and the use of cartoon characters, and the ability for individual smokers to bring their own lawsuits in the future. Because he had pursued the case on a contingent-fee basis, Scruggs stood to gain more than $1 billion from the settlement; however, he agreed to have his fees decided by a national panel of judges. More than collecting a giant fee, Scruggs said, he wanted to help the public, "to really make a difference in the world. It was an inspiration. [Lawyers] got caught up in [the] feeling . . . they were really doing a service to humanity."[9] Currently, Scruggs is fighting insurance companies that have denied payment on thousands of damage claims in the aftermath of Hurricane Katrina. Thus far, he has recovered $130 million from State Farm Insurance to be paid to policyholders in Mississippi.[10]

Lawyers are also at the forefront of the battle over religion in public life and represent both sides of this contentious public debate. In the United States, every citizen has the constitutional right to worship as he or she believes without state interference,

A More Just Society

just as every citizen has the right to be free of state-imposed religious strictures.

- When a school board prohibits a Muslim girl from wearing her head scarf, that school board has just bought an important and public legal dispute.

- If a high school principal refuses to let a Bible study group meet after hours in a schoolroom in which all other school activity clubs are free to meet, that principal is likely to face a courtroom battle.

- When a judge installs a copy of the Ten Commandments in the courtroom, the separation of church and state is put into question.

- If a menorah is displayed on the city hall lawn in the holiday season, but a manger scene cannot be displayed and Christmas carols cannot be sung on public property, just wait for the legal fireworks.

These and other volatile religious issues draw the lines for the proper place of religion in our national life, and lawyers help the courts keep the two constitutional clauses dealing with religion in proper balance. The First Amendment prevents Congress from passing laws that favor an "establishment" of religion or laws that prohibit a citizen's "free exercise" of religious belief. The genius of that great balancing act is to keep our increasingly diverse population and our contentious public debates over religion in good constitutional order.

But zealous lawyer advocacy is not limited to civil, human, or criminal rights. Every day—in zoning hearings, condemnation lawsuits, homeowner association battles, and noise abatement proceedings—lawyers fight vigorously to preserve private property rights.

- When a large developer prevails upon a city council to condemn a homeowner's property so that a new private development can be built, alarm bells ring as to whether there has been a taking of private property without the due process of law and the just compensation explicitly required by the Constitution.[11]

- When an overreaching homeowners' association tries to evict a widow who has failed to clear ice from the sidewalk because of a lengthy hospital stay, you can bet there will be a legal battle.

- When dwellers in an apartment complex cannot sleep on weekends because of loud, raucous parties, and their complaints to the police go unanswered, it is nearly certain that a lawyer will be called on to seek appropriate remedies before city administrative boards.

Lawyers fight vigorously to protect fundamental property rights. Their presence is felt in all the commissions, councils, rule-making bodies, and boards established to deal with virtually every aspect of modern life. Sometimes their presence is not comfortable for public officials. Lawyers force governmental bodies (local, state, tribal, and national) to recognize that they, too, must respect the basic property rights of individual citizens. Lawyers have been called "the grease that keeps society's gears from grinding to a halt." While this may not be the most poetic description of the profession, it is an honest portrayal of what lawyers do. As the number of complex human interactions increases, a certain number of them will inevitably go bad. Those grievances must be resolved. Without lawyers, those problems would fester, and, ultimately, democracy would be weakened.

Much work is left for lawyers and their clients, the work of advocacy. Lawyers do more than argue what the law is—they also argue what the law *should be*. The haunting New Testament declaration that "ye have the poor with you always," while true, is of little comfort to a hungry child, a destitute immigrant, a single mother in a crime-infested neighborhood, or an AIDS patient unable to afford medication. As long as the poor are with us, our obligation to alleviate their suffering and to provide aid will never be lifted. Advocacy is another way in which lawyers make society better.

Today, millions of children are wholly without health insurance—children without a voice or a powerful lobby supporting them. Health care costs are skyrocketing. Elected officials and other public policy makers appear paralyzed, caught between budget crises and the claims by competing bands of lobbyists. Millions of citizens are trapped below the poverty line, struggling to hold down multiple jobs that pay the minimum wage. More young black males are in prison than are attending institutes of higher education. Prison construction costs skyrocket, while lawmakers cut the budgets of drug treatment programs.

This list of unmet needs, and others just as serious, speaks volumes about the challenges still facing our democracy and the leadership of the bench and bar. In many instances, lawyers are also members of those legislatures and councils engaging in cutbacks. But many members of the legal profession work hard and provide much free service to address these problems. Unfortunately, budgets for legal aid clinics remain stable or even shrink while serious legal needs increase and go unserved. Bar associations and individual lawyers are pushing for increased public support. Can lawyers do more? Yes. Should they do more? Yes. But society itself, through compelling public debate, led by skilled advocates on all sides, must shape and finance better solutions to these issues—among which must be legal assistance not only for the poor but also for the middle class. Society pays too high a price for unmet legal needs.

As earlier noted, University of Virginia law professor Calvin Woodard argued that society tolerates the intolerable as long as there appear to be no solutions. But in one of the most affluent societies in the history of the planet, the resource base is immense: there *can* be solutions. Millions of well-motivated citizens want to help. Private charities, aid groups, churches, and organizations can—and must—be mobilized. Not all solutions will be governmental, but governmental policies must be supportive of those who work toward them. And lawyers are, and must continue to be, at the center of these efforts. Today, many lawyers are involved in campaigns to

- promote private giving through enlightened tax policies;

- encourage businesses to establish civic-minded programs and to reward employee volunteers;

- stop predatory practices that exploit the poor; and

- expose and correct bureaucratic lethargy and indifference.

"The moral quality of a civilization," Jerome Frank observed, "is measured by its treatment of the weak and the powerless."[12]

Our American civilization will ultimately be measured by how well we respond to these and similar societal needs. Lawyers, and our legal system, will be judged by the quality of the problem solvers we put on the front lines to create and implement solutions.

Lawyers have an ethical obligation to engage in pro bono work, and each year they provide many hours of free legal services. As members of a licensed monopoly, most lawyers feel a sense of obligation. Legal service movements also provide aid to individuals and causes. For example, the organized bar invented the Interest on Lawyers Trust Accounts (IOLTA) program, which captures small amounts of interest that otherwise would go unclaimed and deposits them in a special account. These funds are then distributed to nonprofit organizations that provide, among other things, legal services to the needy.[13]

Law schools have created hundreds of clinics that not only provide educational and practical experience for students but also offer legal assistance in a variety of areas, from representing the indigent, to helping the elderly receive Social Security benefits, assisting AIDS patients in finding medical treatment, aiding miners with black lung disease, or guarding children from abusive caregivers. These clinics not only help people in genuine need, but they also inculcate the value of service in law students and provide for many affluent students a stark education about real people in crisis. As more and more women and students from minority backgrounds enroll in law schools, they bring with them personal knowledge of the legal needs within their communities. This new and diverse breed of lawyers brings a greater breadth of knowledge along with fresh ideas based on personal experience.

When the Berlin Wall fell and the Soviet empire collapsed, twenty or so former Soviet bloc nations abandoned their collectivist precepts and declared themselves to be democratic market economies. Fledgling democracies with almost no experience at self-governing or implementing democratic norms, much less regulating a free-market economy, were thus launched onto the world stage. These nations looked to the Western world, and particularly to the United States, for examples of how legal systems could protect human rights and the basic dignity of their citizens, of how freedom and capitalism could be balanced.

The American Bar Association coordinated an extraordinary, indeed historic, outreach to those countries emerging from decades of oppression by launching the Central and Eastern European Law Initiative (CEELI). The program sent teams of American lawyers to help with the drafting of new laws and the creation of an independent legal profession. Teams of judges continue to give similar help to the judiciaries of those nations. Teams of law professors and law deans went—and are still going—to help improve the legal educational systems. All of the American participants are volunteer lawyers, judges, and professors who provide this pro bono service in the highest tradition of the legal profession. The ABA operates similar programs in Africa, Asia, and throughout the world.[14]

American lawyers and legal scholars are active participants in the creation of a new global legal order, bringing together diverse ideas and systems. The great democracies have developed two principal models for their legal systems. The British established the common law (or adversary) system, which spread throughout the English-speaking world. It is characterized by the use of the jury, strong advocates employing cross-examination, and a neutral judge. Much of the rest of Europe gravitated to the model established by the Napoleonic code, called the civil law system or inquisitorial model. The civil law system is characterized by a strong judge who interrogates the witnesses and finds the facts, while the lawyers act primarily as fact-gatherers and have a more passive role at trial. There are many versions of the two systems throughout Europe, Africa, Asia, and the Americas, so these descriptions are, of necessity, generalized: because cultures are unique, the wholesale transplanting of systems from one nation to another has proven difficult.

These two models dominate law in the industrialized democracies and their former colonies, the European-style civil law system being far more prevalent than the British common law system. Nevertheless, in part because of widespread exposure to depictions of American legal life through TV, movies, and news media, the American courtroom, with its fact-finding jury and transparent commitment to fairness, has held a certain fascination for the nations emerging from Soviet control.

The former communist countries had something like the civil law system, in which the fact-finding judge asked most of the questions and the more passive lawyers served as gatherers of facts. But in this vastly corrupted system, both prosecutors and defense attorneys were employees of the state, whose first duty was to that state, not to the welfare of their clients. The judges answered directly to high party officials. Bribery and corruption flourished, as did special privilege. The constitutions of those former Soviet states typically guaranteed even more protections than are found in the U.S. Bill of Rights; without an independent bar and an independent judiciary, however, those paper rights were worthless. Is it any wonder that when those systems collapsed, the American version of the adversary system became an attractive alternative? Even if the transfer of specific procedures between systems is too difficult, the fundamental principles on which those procedures are fixed—fairness, transparency, and respect for the rights of the individual—are of universal applicability, and a demonstration of these principles in action can be an invaluable aid to countries struggling to build a just and equitable legal system.

No legal system is perfect; all can be improved. American lawyers are working not only to better the system in the United States but also to assist in improving legal procedures in nations with which we have diplomatic and economic relations. Today, there is enormous interest in perfecting both common law and civil law systems, and the best ideas from each are being discussed and exchanged. For example, joint cooperative educational efforts between Turkish and American law schools have helped with the implementation of new and more just codes and procedures in Turkey. The American experience demonstrates that for fairness and justice to be achieved in any nation, three key elements must be present:

- an independent bar,

- an independent judiciary,

- and a transparency of process.

Without these three ingredients, no legal system in any nation can enjoy the faith and confidence of the citizenry. If the citizens lose faith in the legal system, that system, and the government of which it is a constituent part, runs the risk of stagnation and eventual collapse.

If the same rights are not available to all citizens, it is difficult to maintain the credibility necessary for the continued good functioning of the state. In his review of lawyers' efforts to help create a more just society, Robert A. Stein, former ABA executive director, declared that one of the legal profession's "most important goals is to promote 'access to justice' through expanding 'access to civil legal aid and criminal representation of the poor.'" His conclusion: We are beginning to reach our goals. And, as he subsequently noted, American lawyers are not just working for these goals here in the United States but also helping to achieve them worldwide.[15]

It is inspiring to think of what significant advances have been achieved through law and with the help of lawyers in the post–World War II era.

- Diversity. The legal profession, once the domain of native-born white males, has opened its doors to minorities, women, and immigrant groups. Women, for example, made up less than 10 percent of admitted law students into the late 1960s and early 1970s; today, at least half of all admitted law school students are women. The enrollment of students from racial and ethnic minority groups has also increased dramatically, but there is much more to be done.

- Discrimination. Legislation prohibiting discrimination based on race, religion, ethnic background, gender, sexual orientation, and age has created a whole new field of legal rights and protections and has helped revitalize the promises made in the constitutional amendments ratified after the Civil War.

- Business Abuses. Stock market manipulation, unreasonably dangerous products, false advertising, accounting fraud, predatory pricing, monopolistic practices, credit card scams, and other abusive business practices not only affect individuals but also undermine confidence in the market system on which the nation's economy relies. Lawyers are vigilant in their protection of consumer rights and have been at the forefront of legislative reforms in these areas. It is also true, however, that some lawyers representing businesses have been too close to the heart of the problem.

- Environmental Protection. Our air and water are cleaner, our public lands are better preserved, and our endangered species are safer than they would be without the influence of lawyers, both in the courtroom and in state and federal regulatory agencies. Concern about the environment is now a major national issue, and American lawyers will continue to play an important role in shaping policy solutions.

- Disability Rights. The national focus on the needs of the disabled citizen in the last few years has been laudable—and, again, lawyers have been at the forefront, ensuring compliance with standards for accessibility to public areas.

All of these efforts demonstrate how lawyers and the law change—and can bring about change—for the better. But as these examples also clearly establish, improvement must continue. There is much left to be done. Furthermore, the future will bring new public debate and conflicts—from space law to genetic manipulation, cell research, and bioproperty—which, in turn, must eventually be resolved by new policies.

A More Just Society

Without the great legal reforms of the last century, many crafted and nurtured by lawyers, where would our democracy be? Indeed, our world would be quite different. We would have laborers—many of them poor, uneducated children—working fourteen-hour days for brutally low wages. Our air and water would be more polluted, and our public lands exploited and despoiled. Corporate buccaneers would reign without check, and new generations of Rockefellers, Lays, Dukes, and Vanderbilts would dominate economic life. There would be few stock market controls, few antitrust actions, few consumer protections, few fair employment laws, few antidiscrimination policies, and few protections for the disabled. Without enforcement of the separation between church and state, we might be living under some form of federally recognized religious system conceived by self-styled fundamentalists. Women, gays and lesbians, immigrants, and racial minorities would have little or no protection from majoritarian tyranny: the promise of the equal protection clause would be a hollow joke. And the rights of the accused would depend on the whim of a judge or a prosecutor.

The world is a different place—we think a better one—because lawyers helped work through public debates and extensive litigation on heated policy issues. Lawyers are not necessarily lovable. Lawyers are often contentious, if not obnoxious. It is easy to take shots at the legal profession. Lawyers may bring bad news, but lawyers are nonetheless essential if our democratic society is to survive and prosper. Justice is not self-executing. The playing field is not automatically level. A written Bill of Rights does not guarantee that those rights will be respected. Lawyers help ensure the separation of powers between state and federal authority. Lawyers insist that we respect the checks and balances between the three branches of government. Lawyers demand that the judiciary remain independent. They also strive to maintain an independent bar, able to represent individual citizens. Lawyers fight to ensure that our legal process remains open and transparent and that the economy works for the benefit of society. The American legal system as a human institution is not perfect. It never will be. It can be improved. Indeed, it must be improved. We believe even greater reform is not only possible, but imperative. Such reform is the great challenge for lawyers and legal educators, most especially for the coming generation of new lawyers.

Stanford professor Deborah Rhode, former president of the Association of American Law Schools, focuses upon the need for reform in her thoughtful study, *In the Interest of Justice: Refining the Legal Profession* (2000).[16] She argues that real reform cannot occur until lawyers focus directly on such questions as inequality, alternative dispute resolution, lack of access to services, high cost of litigation, lawyer maldistribution, availability of funding, licensing, and disciplinary regulatory response. Rhode reminds readers of William Ralph Inge's observation that "it is useless for the sheep to pass resolutions in favor of vegetarianism while the wolf remains of a different opinion." Her conclusion is nevertheless affirming:

[T]he obstacles to reform are by no means insurmountable. Lawyers have been in the forefront of every major movement for social justice in American history, and their efforts have been a model throughout the world. The bar has made dramatic progress in addressing many issues of professional responsibility. . . . At a time of widespread dissatisfaction with many aspects of lawyers' work, it does not seem unrealistic to hope that some of the bar's best instincts could be re-channeled toward more fundamental change. . . . The challenge now is to enlist both the public and the profession in reforms that will reconnect the ideals and the institutions of legal practice.[17]

Simply because, as we argue, lawyers are not the primary cause of the discontents in twenty-first-century America does not mean that the legal profession can ignore, dismiss, or escape them. Nor does it reduce our professional obligation to address their resolution. We are not the first to live in such a difficult age. There is a marvelous Hogarth illustration entitled "Credulity, Superstition and Fanaticism," which seems to be every bit as descriptive of the twenty-first century as of the eighteenth century in which it was executed.[18] It depicts a church service gone mad, presided over by demagogues using all manner of chicanery to cow the credulous masses. We, as a people, have been led to believe that we can conquer economic dislocation, control unemployment and inflation, fight foreign wars, grant tax cuts, build a massive national debt, expend personal and federal dollars to prevent recession while exporting jobs and importing goods. We have been all too willing to ignore massive consumption of limited reserves in a time of global warming, family breakups, drug abuse, and the breakdown of historic values.

Lawyers, as leaders, have an obligation to face reality and to help bring about necessary reforms. But when lawyers press forward for resolution of these issues, they become identified with—indeed blamed for—the problems themselves. However, we are not talking about lawyers acting exclusively in their courtroom role. Instead, we are exploring what earlier generations of legal and political science scholars called "the public policy role of lawyering." It is the challenge that Woodard called "merging tradition and reality." We are calling for what we earlier denominated as the balancing task of accommodating continuity and change.

If our civilization is to survive, lawyers must be more than mere mechanics. They must be ready to be referees and reconcilers. The Spanish philosopher José Ortega y Gasset, who early warned us of mass man and the dangers of mass society, introduced what he called "the concept of generations." He proclaims that generations have tasks and that, tragically, many of them are not up to their task.[19] We believe the task of this upcoming generation of lawyers is to free us from the iron grip of the clash of different traditions and to bring us face-to-face with the reality of this changed and changing world.

Unless society acknowledges that we all must reach beyond what newscasters and political commentators tell us, unless we are willing to reject the untested tenets of the popular Left or Right, then we have nothing to look forward to but a continuation of this Hogarthian madhouse in which we live. It is not enough to hold what we are told are the right views and the right causes. We must ask—indeed demand to know—why these are correct views and correct causes. To accept the assertion of popular press and culture is particularly dangerous in this time of rapid change. The danger of culture lag is too great; the challenge of balancing continuity and change is too compelling.

We began this book with a strong defense of lawyers, examining the antiattorney myths of the popular press. We then explored the emergence of lawyer bashing as contemporary sport. Stories in modern news magazines and cable news channels have about a three-week cycle, resulting in a world of fortnightly crisis divided into fifteen-minute units of fame. The media have given us a devil-angel theory of law and life inhabited by amoral lawyers and politically motivated judges. Well, it just ain't so! Justice is not black and white, good guys and bad guys, devils and angels. Neither lawyers nor judges are the demons of our age.

The demand for reform in the legal profession, as articulated by Professor Rhode, is as clear as the media distortion of the lawyers' role in the creation of the crisis of our modern age. The challenge for modern lawyers is to rise to the generational task and break out of this mold, to free us from the limitation of the age, and to lead us from the age of credulity, superstition, and fanaticism into an age of reality, reason, and common sense.

Among the needed reforms are more vigorous self-policing by the bar itself; greater access to law and lawyering regardless of income, race, and class; better education for the general public on legal rights and their enforcement; broader and more varied options for dispute resolution; and better opportunities for legal education among those underrepresented in the profession. Earlier, we called for the establishment of a moratorium on radical experiments and for special commissions to address how law and lawyers deal with change. This is perhaps the greatest challenge facing those of us who are law school deans, professors, or judges—those of us to whom this task is ideally suited. It is also a primary responsibility of the practicing bar. America's lawyers must continue to be the leaders of reform.

We set forth here what we believe are commonsense suggestions for improvement of the legal profession and its relationship to American society, an agenda for the next generation of lawyers. Although we have described lawyers as society's agents of change, we must acknowledge that changing the legal profession's norms, entrenched practices, and mind-sets will be every bit as difficult as achieving reform elsewhere in society. We have divided our proposals into four segments: suggestions for the bar, the judiciary, the law schools, and the public.

A Reform Agenda for the Bar

ALL FORMS OF BILLING FOR SERVICES MUST BE IMPROVED, AND METHODS OF POLICING ABUSES MUST BE STREAMLINED.

The lawyer-client relationship begins with what is essentially an inherent conflict of interest: the lawyer wants to earn as much as possible, and the client wants to pay as little as possible. The contingent fee provides access to the courts, but it also lends itself to serious abuse. Billing by the hour, the hourly fee, is subject to a myriad of ways to inflate the actual hours spent on productive work. Clients must have a forum in which they can challenge fees, a forum that is readily available, impartial, responsive, and open.

THE BAR DISCIPLINARY PROCESS MUST BE INDEPENDENT, WELL-FUNDED, AND MORE TRANSPARENT.

We firmly believe that the lawyer disciplinary process in most states is more efficient, that the imposition of sanctions is more regularized, and that lawyers' ethical codes are more comprehensive than are the comparable processes for any other profession. Medicine lags far behind, and the other professions trail even further back. As for the press and the clergy, forget it! But the bar can do much better. More lay members should be appointed to disciplinary panels. Earlier acknowledgment to the public of complaints should be considered. For example, the North Carolina bar began looking into the actions of prosecutor Mike Nifong of Durham, North Carolina, in the infamous Duke

A More Just Society

Lacrosse case. They did this within a few weeks after complaints of prosecutorial misconduct surfaced, but the public was not aware that a responsible body was actually looking into the matter. In the interim, public confidence understandably eroded in the bar's ability to police itself.[20]

THE BAR'S ETHICAL CODE, THE MODEL RULES OF PROFESSIONAL CONDUCT, MUST REGULARLY BE REVIEWED AND UPDATED TO BALANCE THE LAWYERS' COMPETING DUTIES OF LOYALTY TO THE CLIENT AND FIDELITY TO THE LEGAL SYSTEM.

With very few exceptions, under the attorney-client privilege, a lawyer must zealously guard a client's confidences while avoiding deceptive conduct before a court or any fraudulent acts that will injure the public. The lawyer is, after all, an officer of the court. Enron and other corporate scandals demonstrate the need for diligence in balancing these competing duties.

VIGOROUS AND SUSTAINED EFFORTS TO EXPAND AND IMPROVE THE AVAILABILITY OF LEGAL SERVICES TO UNDERSERVED SEGMENTS OF SOCIETY MUST BE AT THE FOREFRONT OF THE BAR'S AGENDA.

Public funding for legal services must receive more emphasis as well as more taxpayer dollars. The bar must emphasize the duty to provide pro bono services and work to expand the number of attorneys providing such services. The need is so great that *mandatory* pro bono requirements may be necessary. Why shouldn't a lawyer be required to provide fifty or a hundred hours of free services a year in order to retain her or his monopoly license to practice law? Law students already engage in such mandatory activities in an increasing number of law schools.

The formal trial should remain the last resort. The bench and bar must support and encourage negotiation, mediation, arbitration, and other less costly and less time-consuming ways of settling disputes. The recent emergence of such programs should be built upon to resolve many of the complaints against lawyers and the legal process.

A Reform Agenda for the Judiciary

OUR METHODS OF SELECTING JUDGES MUST BE
EVALUATED AND IMPROVED.

There is simply no excuse for selecting judges in partisan political elections. Long ballot lists of judicial candidates, designated as Democrat or Republican, are simply wrong: the public cannot know the candidates individually and can vote only on the basis of political persuasion. The people who contribute to such judicial campaigns are too often those who will appear before the judges. One would be hard pressed to come up with a worse system.

The fight for reform in Texas is instructive. The former chief justice of the Texas Supreme Court, Thomas R. Phillips, rebelled against the Texas system of partisan political election of judges throughout his long tenure (1988–2004). In his first campaign in 1988, Phillips became the first successful Texas Supreme Court candidate in modern times to place voluntary limits on the size of campaign contributions. Later, he led the court to amend the Texas Code of Judicial Conduct to limit the time during which contributions could be accepted and to require greater disclosure of contribution records. These initiatives formed the basis for later legislative reform. During his fourth and final campaign in 2002, Phillips refused to accept any contributions from any source. Phillips had less success with his efforts to change the system of partisan political elections. Despite overwhelming support from the press and bar and repeated success in the Texas Senate, leadership in the Texas House of Representatives never allowed the necessary constitutional amendment to come to a floor vote. The simple fact is that both political parties, the one in power and the one wanting to be in power, have a vested interest in putting forth partisan slates of judges in future elections. They and their political consultants have kept Texas in the backwater of judicial reform.[21]

The federal system of presidential judicial appointments and Senate confirmation, with lifetime job security during good behavior, is substantially better. Yet the public has been exposed to an appalling level of partisan bickering and political payback in the confirmation process, enough to bring a good system into disrepute. The president might consider forming public panels of highly respected professionals to screen and recommend names for nominations. Lastly, the Senate—and this means the senators from both parties—must take politics out of judicial appointments. The ABA's role in vetting the qualifications of federal court candidates has been highly praised but very often ignored.

THERE SHOULD BE MANDATORY JUDICIAL EDUCATIONAL PROGRAMS
AFTER SELECTION AND PRIOR TO TAKING THE BENCH.

Under the present system, a lawyer who has been in a business practice for many years may be elected or appointed to the bench, sworn in, and the next day find herself judging a complex criminal case or a domestic matter. We are confident that new judges would welcome an opportunity for judicial education and mentoring and that experienced judges would be willing to provide guidance and expertise for such programs. Other countries, such as Brazil and Germany, require far more preparation for the judiciary.

THE PROCESS OF JUDICIAL DISCIPLINE NEEDS

ADDITIONAL REGULARIZATION AND TRANSPARENCY.

Judges are human and are subject to the general frailties of our species. The judiciary must be responsive to a more open process to hear and act on complaints of judicial misconduct, which today often goes unnoticed or undisciplined.

A Reform Agenda for Law Schools

LAW SCHOOLS SHOULD USE THEIR RESOURCES FOR IMPROVING

LEGAL EDUCATION AND NOT FOR PUBLIC RELATIONS.

The excessive preoccupation of many deans and faculty members with the *U.S. News and World Report* annual law school rankings has led to misuse of resources, reduction of minority access to legal education, and charges of outright cheating by some deans. The law schools, the American Bar Association and its Section on Legal Education, the Association of American Law Schools, and the Law School Admissions Council have a critical stake in the avoidance of such abusive and costly practices. They also have an obligation to consumers of legal education to report accurately on the state of their law schools. Questionable activities of offending law schools should be exposed, and accreditation sanctions considered. And *U.S. News and World Report* should be ashamed of itself for failing to understand that what is the best law school for one student may not be the best for another.

CLINICAL PROGRAMS, PRO BONO REQUIREMENTS, AND EFFORTS TO
DIVERSIFY THE STUDENT BODIES OF AMERICAN LAW SCHOOLS
SHOULD REMAIN PRIORITY ITEMS.

Such programs not only better prepare students for practice and expose them to society's needs, but they also help society's most vulnerable members find access to needed legal services. Furthermore, loan forgiveness programs that reduce the financial obligations of graduates who perform public service should be expanded. In September 2007, a loan forgiveness program was signed by the president; while this is helpful, there is still much left to be done. Law students should be treated equitably in comparison to students in other professions; this includes congressional support for loan repayment programs that are on a par with those offered to students of medicine.

INNOVATIVE EFFORTS TO PROVIDE TEACHING OPPORTUNITIES FOR
THE BEST AND BRIGHTEST YOUNG LAWYERS MUST BE UNDERTAKEN.

The increase in human longevity, coupled with tenure and the abolition of mandatory retirement ages, has resulted in the graying of law school faculties and a reduction in the availability of new teaching positions. In the face of a rapidly increasing and attractive pool of bright, energetic young teachers with new ideas, we must figure out ways to open the legal education profession to them—for example, by expanding legal education to the undergraduate or even high school levels.

LAW SCHOOLS SHOULD ACTIVELY PARTICIPATE IN EFFORTS TO REQUIRE
THE HIGHEST STANDARDS OF PERFORMANCE FOR LEGAL EDUCATION.

It is particularly appropriate that well-financed and highly respected law schools should seek to serve as role models, exercising a leadership role in defining best practices and creating innovative programs. They should join in elevating standards rather than fighting to lower them for selfish, parochial interests designed to advance their own agendas. They can help ensure that broad ideas, not technically focused and minimally restrictive rules, govern accreditation.

A Reform Agenda for the Public

AMERICANS MUST STRIVE TO IMPROVE THEIR KNOWLEDGE AND UNDERSTANDING OF OUR DEMOCRACY, OUR GOVERNMENT, OUR COURT SYSTEM, AND OUR BASIC RIGHTS.

This idea is both simple and obvious, but of the highest priority. Elementary schools, middle schools, high schools, and colleges must do a better job of teaching the basics of how our legal system works. The organized bar, judiciary, and law schools should engage in serious and continuous outreach to help in this task.

THE MEDIA MUST ADOPT A CODE OF INDUSTRY PRACTICES IN THEIR COVERAGE OF LEGAL ISSUES.

This code should require that the media give a full explanation of a case and the unfolding facts as they occur. No longer should it be possible to introduce a case with provocative headlines and then ignore later facts and the ultimate outcome. This suggestion might be called a press version of the witnesses' oath: "Tell the truth, the whole truth, and nothing but the truth."

THE PUBLIC MUST BE PREPARED TO FUND AN ADEQUATE JUDICIAL SYSTEM.

Justice does not come cheap. Failure to adequately fund a judicial system costs more in the long run. Pay now, or pay more

A More Just Society

later—not only in dollars, but in human tragedy. The public must be prepared to fund more judges, more public defenders, more drug rehabilitation centers, and better forensic labs, among other things.

In concluding this chapter, let us return to Peter Marshall and his keeper of the spring. The waters of the stream brought life, commerce, and tourists. And the keeper of the spring ensured that the spring was clean, clear, and free flowing. If keepers are dismissed or unduly restricted, disaster will occur. But even if all our keepers are kept at work, the additional strain of change will require not fewer, but more and better guardians—new and more dedicated keepers, soldiers, builders, and healers.

In the classic movie *It's a Wonderful Life* (1946), we are asked what Bedford Falls would be like if the character George Bailey had never been born. Let us ask ourselves where we would be had there been no American lawyers—no Thomas Jefferson, John Adams, James Madison, John Marshall, Abraham Lincoln, Clarence Darrow, Thurgood Marshall, Felix Frankfurter, Felix Cohen, John Minor Wisdom, Frank Minis Johnson, Earl Warren, James P. White, Sandra Day O'Connor, or Ruth Bader Ginsburg? All of these are heroic lawyers—all, in their own way, keepers of our democracy's springs, foot soldiers of the Constitution, and healers of the body politic.

When he was a young man, U.S. Supreme Court Justice Hugo Black was a member of the Ku Klux Klan; at the end of his life, he was considered the architect of key decisions that applied the Bill of Rights protections that bind federal actions and made them applicable to state governments. He is said to have mused that in his life he traded in the white robes of hate for the black robes of justice. "As a young man," Black is reported to have observed, "I put on white robes and scared blacks; as an old man I put on black robes and scared whites."[22]

Just as an individual can grow and change, so our system grows and changes. Every day, America's lawyers fight new battles in the courtrooms of the land and in the chambers of the policy makers. Law is a question of enforcing majority rule while respecting minority rights; it is a question of protecting individual dignity, while respecting communitarian values. Battles are won and lost in our great democracy, but battles must constantly be fought. And every day, the spring must be cleansed by our professional problem solvers, the American lawyers.

One of our colleagues, in hearing about this book, called the work "Three Cheers for the Lawyer." And in many ways we intend it to be exactly that—a no-holds-barred defense of lawyers and lawyering. Actually, we think of it more as two and a half cheers because, while we focus on the positive, we acknowledge the struggle to improve the profession and the need for reforms as well as the all-too-many lapses, inadequacies, and downright failures of the profession.

Nonetheless, whether one thinks of them as keepers of the springs, foot soldiers of the Constitution, architects and carpenters of commerce, umpires and field levelers, healers of the body politic, or simply bridge builders, lawyers are essential to American democracy. Even if one sees lawyers as sharks, beavers, or ambulance chasers, they still keep society on track, and without them, change would be more difficult and misdirected. As Alexis de Tocqueville observed almost two centuries ago, "When the American people are intoxicated by passion or carried away by the impetuosity of their ideas, they are checked by the almost invisible influence of their legal counselors."[23] In the final analysis, in a nation committed to the rule of law, lawyers remain indispensable.

WORDS FOR THE NEXT GENERATION
OF AMERICA'S LAWYERS

Our concluding chapter is intended primarily for the upcoming generation of new lawyers, for those thinking about the study of law. For readers who are already lawyers or judges, it is our hope that we have helped renew your commitment to our great profession. Every day, your devotion to the lawyers' tasks makes our Constitution and the rule of law live. For our lay readers, we genuinely hope that we have given you a better understanding and appreciation of the role of law and the legal profession in our rapidly changing democracy. This final note, our postscript, is written for that highly committed young woman or man who asks, "Should I become a lawyer?"[1] In some ways, this is the benediction of our sermon on America's lawyers, a call for a new generation to come forth and do likewise.

When you mentioned to family or friends you were considering becoming a lawyer, you may have faced skepticism, if not serious criticism. You may have heard such comments as, "How can you defend someone you know is guilty?" "Lawyers feed off of the woes of others!" "Lawyer nitpicking raises the cost of everything!" You are undoubtedly asking yourself whether three or four years of rigorous and costly legal education are really worth the candle. For you, from whom must come our next generation of lawyers, we add these final comments. We hope they will help reassure you, as well as your friends and family, that it is possible, as Oliver Wendell Holmes Jr. proclaimed, "to live greatly in the law."[2]

The legal profession is essential to our democracy; it is a profession, a career, you should not fear. Indeed, it is a career that many will probably embrace. However, it is not a place for the weak of heart or the reluctant. A good legal education is an exceptional preparation for a multiplicity of vital roles in our society. As the lawyer and theatrical producer Victor Cook observed, "A lawyer has a backstage pass to the concert of life."[3]

Law school vastly improves the skills of critical thinking, analysis, and communication. You can prepare for a wide variety of legal specialties and other tasks that are both extremely interesting and of great service. You can venture beyond law into business, government, charitable works, and, yes, even politics and entertainment. No profession better equips you to confront the increasingly rapid changes society faces. Remember, lawyers are on every side of every proposed change, struggling to ensure that the change is well considered and that when it is made, all proceeds peacefully within an ordered democratic structure.

A famous Chinese curse, perhaps the truest cliché of our age, most certainly applies to twenty-first-century lawyers: "May you live in interesting times." If you choose to study law during the next three to four years, you will study interesting topics in interesting times. All around you, legal issues dominate the public agenda on both the national and international stages. A good legal education is more that challenging: it is fascinating and invaluable.

Three simple but enduring words will make you not only a good student but a great lawyer as well. Should you decide to become a lawyer, these words should be your polestar. They are: competency, responsiveness, and integrity.

Competency

At the heart of the word competency is the ability to take control of one's own time, one's own life, and one's own career. And the time for taking control of your destiny is now, as you contemplate whether to study law. Too many in this society are what the Cherokee-Creek artist Joan Hill called "children of the elements"—people whose lives are not planned, not thought out—individuals who live only by the expediency of the moment.[4] As T. S. Eliot wrote in his play *The Confidential Clerk*, "Sir, if you haven't the strength to impose your own terms upon life, you must accept the terms it offers you."[5]

Competency for a lawyer means a lifelong commitment to providing high-quality professional service to society, as well as to one's clients, and to the resolution of the issues of one's age. You start that process of becoming competent by how you decide to use your time in law school. Being a competent lawyer is hard work, and no one should select this career without an appreciation and understanding of how long that work goes on.

There is a story told by Dr. Andy Watson, an MD as well as a lawyer, who taught at the University of Michigan. He called himself a "psychologist for the legal community." Speaking to a group of law school spouses, he entitled his talk "Don't You Believe Them." The gist of his advice to the young spouses or partners of first-year law students was, "It never gets easier." He asserted that the future lawyer would tell them that it will "get better" after "the first year in law school, and then better after law review try-outs, better after graduation, better after passing the bar, better after partnership, better after the next case and, finally, better after retirement."[6] Lawyering is hard but rewarding work that never gets easier. Therefore, it is with malice aforethought that educators have created a legal education system that is also hard work. If you make the decision to study law, you must also make the decision to work hard in law school and be prepared to deal with a career of hard work.

No matter how good the motive, one does no service for clients—white, black, brown, red, or green—if the service provided is second-rate. And that is true no matter what kind of law you practice. You can't be a good poverty lawyer simply because you have been poor or because you sympathize with the poor and the downtrodden. Every legal task bears the stamp of your identity and carries your reputation. We urge you to do each task in law school and beyond as well as you can, and upon completion, evaluate your performance at each task. Constantly seeking to improve is the good lawyers' way.

Responsiveness

To live the life of the modern lawyer requires an affirmation, a commitment, a willingness to speak up. As a lawyer, you will often

Words for the Next Generation

be in the center of controversy and subject to attack by the public press. You must search for what Thomas Carlyle called "our duty and our destiny." Lawyers must ponder ultimate questions—questions about what we think we *ought* to be, about what our lives ought to count for. Socrates said, "The unexamined life is not worth living." In order to be truly responsive to the inner voice that guides you, then you must follow those fundamental values that you hope to preserve. Near the conclusion of Thomas Wolfe's autobiographical novel, *Look Homeward, Angel,* the young hero calls out to the ghost of his brother Ben, "Where is my world, what is my life to be?" And Ben replies, "You are your world."[7]

To truly respond to the needs of others, you must know and respond to your own best impulses. No less a lawyer's lawyer than Harlan Fiske Stone has warned that "law is neither formal logic nor the embodiment of inexorable scientific laws. It is a human institution, created by human agents to serve human ends."[8] And Justice Felix Frankfurter went further to warn that "lawyers better remember that they are human beings, and a human being who hasn't had . . . periods of doubts and disappointment must be a cabbage, not a human being."[9] In short, if you choose to be a lawyer, make a commitment, an affirmation; be ready to stand up for what you believe to be right. Do not be indifferent. Recognize that in the law, there is often right and wrong and that it is wrong not to stand for what is right. As Dante reminded us, "The hottest places in hell are reserved for those who remain neutral in a time of great moral crisis."[10] And surely, these are such times.

But we must add a special word of caution for the prospective law student: to be responsive—to respond to our best inner impulses—does not mean that we must be dogmatic or dictatorial.

It certainly does not mean that we can be intolerant of the deeply held views of others, even those that may differ from our own. Good law schools nurture a sense of community that respects and values diverse backgrounds, beliefs, religions, and viewpoints. Law school is a very special place. You will meet friends in law school who will remain your friends for life. You will learn to value, respect, and love others, even when their views and backgrounds are radically different from your own. Law schools are committed to maintaining basic rights, including First Amendment values. The ability of each to express his or her own views is crucial in the development of legal professionals. Be tolerant of views of others. You will learn as a lawyer that behaving intolerantly in the name of furthering tolerance never advances one's own cause or the goals of a civilized society.

Integrity

This is the most important word of the three. Lawyers can be highly competent. Lawyers can be responsive to human needs as they see them. But if lawyers can't be trusted, then all is lost. Your reputation as a professional is, in the final analysis, all you have. There is simply no substitute for honesty, for the belief that the lawyer's word is his or her bond. An old Texas judge told a group of newly admitted attorneys that he had only one overriding five-word rule in his court: "Be straight, or be gone." We can't add to that. And the profession you are hoping to enter must be even more vigilant in enforcing these standards upon itself.

As you consider your decision to become a lawyer, you should take a moment to reexamine your motives for selecting law. It is frequently alleged that too many young people are brought to law school by three wrong motives: money, prestige, and power.

It is not hyperbole to suggest that those motives, if pursued unchecked, will prostitute this profession, destroy your personal reputations, and bring great disservice to the public. At this point, let us lecture you with a short, professional sermonette. Don't ever forget that lawyers are professionals in a calling whose very roots lie in human rights, public service, and governmental reform. As a lawyer you stand in the shoes of others whom you are sworn to protect. You represent them, and as their representative are obligated to deliver your best. Service and reform in the cause of humanity, not the motives of money, prestige, or power, should remain your highest goals. If so, you will walk the trail blazed by giant after giant after giant of the legal profession. We urge you to read about these heroic legal predecessors.

One of our beloved colleagues, South Texas College of Law professor Charles Weigel, who passed away in 2006, concluded every semester's final class session by describing how he had been transformed by the law. Before entering law school, Weigel served as a naval officer during World War II and helped search the Bataan Death March trails for the graves of American soldiers. The experience ingrained in him a deep hatred of the Japanese. Later, as a law student, Weigel embarked on a research study of the Japanese war crimes trials. According to Weigel, General Douglas MacArthur and his aides chose defense counsel for the Japanese charged with perpetration of war crimes from the ranks of officers who had just come out of battle. These high-level commanders intended the junior officers to do little more than read the case files and show up for trial.

The young defense counselors surprised their superiors by asking for time and resources to mount a vigorous defense for their clients. As a result, these defense lawyers were disparaged, discouraged, and denied promotion. Despite being so deeply and bitterly engaged with their sworn enemy during the war—and being faced with the atrocities that their own clients had committed—the lawyers raised money out of their own pockets to prepare and file a writ of certiorari in the Japanese prisoners' defense. Weigel ended his last day of each semester by reading a letter to one of the former defense counselors from one of the defendants, a captain in the imperial Japanese army: "It is my great pleasure to express my thanks to you for your effort that you rendered to me during my trial . . . . I think there are some wonderful things that we Japanese must learn from your country and I am very glad to tell you that I found one beautiful thing through you . . . . I pray for you and prosperity of your future." Where did defense counsel's dedication and belief come from? Weigel told his students that it was because these officers had been trained as lawyers to believe that they had a noble profession and obligation. These American combat officers were Weigel's heroes, and he left his students with a charge to do the same, to represent their clients, no matter who they were, with capability, dignity, honor, and courage.[11]

We hope that as you enter your career as a lawyer, you take in stride both the criticisms and the compliments as well as the money and the prestige and the power that often come to a good lawyer. Most lawyers have upheld the honor of the profession. We are reminded in these days of verbal attacks on law and lawyers as well as judges, of the oft-quoted words of Harrison Tweed, "I have a high opinion of lawyers. With all their faults, they stack up well against those of every other occupation or profession. They are better to work with or play with or fight with or drink with, than most other varieties of mankind."[12]

Why then these three words? Why do we want you to remember competency, responsiveness, and integrity when you select a legal career? Those words are what we mean when we call for professional excellence. The commitment to affirm lifetime goals of excellence does not always mean you will succeed in a worldly sense. Nevertheless, professional excellence means more than simply acquiring money, power, or the trinkets of an affluent civilization. Remember that excellence does not require, in the name of zealous advocacy, the surrender—the selling out—of one's conscience.

You will bring with you to the study and practice of law your own and your family's highest values, traditions, and goals. Hopefully, law school will strengthen them as well as open you to new and stronger goals of fairness and justice. In the early days of the American Indian Law Scholarship program at the University of New Mexico, director P. Sam Deloria was confronted by a group of Native American prelaw students who were fearful that law school might change them into something or someone they were not. Sam, with a razor-edged sense of humor to match a deep sense of traditional Native values, responded, "You remember your cousin who went away to the Bureau of Indian Affairs trade school to study auto mechanics. Well, he didn't come back as a 1967 Ford, did he? Law school won't make you into an ambulance-chasing shyster either. You are the one whose conscience you must and will follow." Law school will help you refine and reaffirm, indeed build upon, values that are important to you. Being a lawyer gives you an opportunity to actualize your values in ways that strengthen society.

The great Lakota Sioux warrior, Crazy Horse, one of our first environmentalists, said in 1875, "One does not sell the land people walk on."[13] Likewise, a lawyer committed to the true meaning of excellence does not sell out the ethics on which she stands or upon which his profession was founded. Excellence means commitment to truth-seeking, truth-telling, and honest dealing. It means achieving at the highest possible level of competence. This is a lifelong personal and professional challenge. We hope, as you seriously consider this profession, that you make your decision with full knowledge of the difficulties and opportunities ahead. For it is to America's lawyers that democracy turns in times such as ours, when historic ideas and new realities clash. There is no more ennobling profession than this one. Law allows you to serve as society's keepers of the springs and foot soldiers of the Constitution.

In conclusion, let us return to Oliver Wendell Holmes Jr., the great jurist whom we both quoted in our first-year law student orientation speeches of chapter 1. Near the conclusion of his service to the Supreme Court, he recalled his own father, the great New England literary figure known as "the autocrat of the breakfast table." When young Holmes finally recovered from his third wound suffered in the Civil War, he decided to return to law school because the army said it had no further need of him. He rushed into his father's study and blurted out, "I am going to the law school." Whereupon Doctor Holmes looked up from his book and declared, "What's the use of that Wendell? A lawyer cannot be a great man."[14]

It seems to be in direct refutation of his father that Holmes wrote that "one could live as greatly in the law as well as elsewhere." At ninety, the justice remarked that his father had "kicked him upstairs into the law" and that he ought to be grateful. Those, like the autocratic Doctor Holmes, who discourage sons, daughters, and friends from considering the law, forget that whether you are a physician or a barrister or even a television commentator, it is your own moral character that guides you in your profession.

There is a wonderful Native American tale that illustrates the point. A smart-aleck Indian boy determined to outsmart the tribal elder who was universally regarded as the wisest of men. The boy took a small bird from its nest and held it in his hand. He sought out the wise man and asked him, "Is this bird dead or alive?" If the man said, "Alive," he planned to crush it in his hands. If he said, "Dead," then he would let it fly away. The wise old man looked him in the eyes and said, "It is as you will." And so it is with a profession. You choose how you will live your life, what level of greatness you bring to it.

In the final analysis, law school is a professional education designed to prepare lawyers for a role in society. A thoughtful warning on the opportunity and limitations of the experience is contained in an early Stanford University Law School bulletin.

> Lawyers are not Philosopher Kings to whom the rest of society looks and defers for substantive answers to [all] problems. And students who go to law school thinking that it will train them to be Philosopher Kings make a serious error and will be sorely disappointed. But lawyers are among the most active participants in the process of working out accommodations and solutions to human problems; for the first-class lawyer is an unusually productive mix of technician, analyst, gladiator, counselor, tactician, institutional architect, politician and scholar. Lawyers trained today will be called upon to help work out the new laws and new legal institutions that will be needed tomorrow and to protect the lives and freedoms of people caught up in a changing, crowded world.[15]

ACKNOWLEDGMENTS

The authors are deeply in the debt of those members of the legal profession whose conduct has given the lie to so many of the common lawyer myths regularly repeated by the antilawyer press and politicians. We are equally grateful to the dozens of our professional colleagues—teachers, judges, and practitioners—with whom we have discussed the ideas set forth in this book.

Our greatest sense of gratitude is reserved for our Swallow Press / Ohio University Press editors, who challenged our concepts and carefully edited our words. Ricky S. Huard, who served as our project editor, is a lawyer, and his legal understanding and knowledge are reflected throughout the book. Gillian Berchowitz, senior editor of the press, was especially helpful in assisting us with the structural reorganization of the manuscript.

Our research was greatly assisted by three students: current law students Christiana Biggs and Barbara Gwinn, and Michael McLellan, who is now a member of the Oregon Bar. We were, as always, guided by our law librarians—Darin Fox, of the University of Oklahoma, and Dennis Hyatt and Mary Ann Hyatt, of the University of Oregon. We were strongly supported by our deans, who appreciated what we felt compelled to write: James J. Alfini, president and dean of South Texas College of Law; Andrew Coats, dean and director of the University of Oklahoma Law Center, and his associate deans, Michael Scaperlanda and

William M. Tabb; and Margie Paris, dean of the University of Oregon School of Law, and her associate deans, Susan Gary and Jane Gordon.

We would particularly like to thank the following colleagues, who provided detailed comments and careful asides as we worked through our defense of the American legal profession: Taunya Banks, Victor Cook, Garrett Epps, Thomas R. Phillips, Steven R. Smith, Mark Steiner, Jerry Thorn, and Ed Wade. The quality of the manuscript was substantially improved by the careful reading and sharp pencils of Nancy Haynes and Peter Winograd.

Leaders of the major national legal education associations visited with us about many of the ideas in our book, and we are most appreciative of their willingness to share their candid thoughts and helpful insights. These include Anne Brandt, Kent Lollis, Phil Shelton, and Joan Van Tol, of the Law School Admission Council; Judith Areen, Jane LaBarbera, Carl Monk, and Nancy Rogers, of the Association of American Law Schools; Bucky Askew, Camille deJorne, Dan Freehling, Randy Hertz, Elizabeth Lacy, Ruth McGregor, William Rakes, Robert Stein, James P. White, and the section council members of the Section on Legal Education and Admission to the Bar of the American Bar Association; and James Leipold, of the National Association for Law Placement.

Donna Williamson, executive assistant at the University of Oregon, worked for five years revising and reformatting the book. At South Texas, invaluable secretarial assistance was provided by Jennifer Hudson, Cindi Lowrimore, and Terri May. Special thanks go to Carol Read, whose dedication to the book has been an inspiration to the authors. We thank Carol with a deep sense of sincere appreciation for her willingness to step in on weekends to take control of the often contrary computers and printers needed to produce our book.

NOTES

Chapter 1

1. As cited in Rennard Strickland, *How to Get into Law School* (New York: Hawthorn, 1974), 11.

2. Kristin Jass Armstrong, "20th Anniversary of the Ryan White Case," *Valpo Lawyer* (Spring 2006): 3.

3. Ibid., 3–5.

4. Data and examples collected by the Law and Popular Culture seminars conducted by Rennard Strickland, University of Oregon School of Law, 2003, 2004, 2005, 2006. See Anthony Chase, "Lawyers and Popular Culture: A Review of Mass Media Portrayals of American Attorneys," *American Bar Foundation Research Journal*, no. 2 (Spring 1986): 281–300. See also Rennard Strickland, Teree Foster, and Taunya Banks, eds., *Screening Justice: The Cinema of Law* (Buffalo, NY: William S. Hein, 2006).

5. In an effort to gather current statistical information, online sources were frequently used. See generally, Eric Moller, *Trends in Civil Jury Verdicts Since 1985* (Santa Monica, CA: Rand Institute for Social Justice, 1996). For this section, information was also gathered from multiple pages at *U.S. Courts*, http://www.uscourts.gov/.

6. Strickland, *How to Get into Law School*, 10–11.

7. "I'll Take That Case," in Charles M. Schultz, *See You Later, Litigator* (San Francisco: Collins, 1996), n.p.

8. Lawrence M. Friedman, *Law in America: A Short History* (New York: Modern Library, 2002), 168. For a brief review of the fields of law, see Wendy Margolis, Bonnie Gordon, and David Rosenlieb, eds., *ABA LSAC Official Guide to ABA-Approved Law Schools*, 2008 ed. (Newtown, PA: Law School Admission Council, 2007).

9. *The New Yorker Book of Lawyer Cartoons* (New York: Alfred A. Knopf, 2005), 63.

10. Quoted in Bruce Nash and Allan Zullo, eds., *Lawyer's Wit and Wisdom: Quotations on the Legal Profession, in Brief* (Philadelphia: Running Press 1995), 168.

11. James G. Leipold, statement, Mid-Year ABA Dean's Conference, Miami, FL, February 9, 2007. See generally the Web site of the National Association for Law Placement, http://www.nalp.org.

12. Quoted in Elizabeth Frost-Knappman and David S. Shrager, eds., *A Concise Encyclopedia of Legal Quotations* (New York: Barnes and Noble Books, 2003), 192.

13. Quoted ibid., 197.

14. Peter Marshall, *Mr. Jones, Meet the Master: Sermons and Prayers of Peter Marshall*, ed. Catherine Marshall (Old Tappan, NJ: Revell Spire, 1980).

15. Alexis de Tocqueville, *Democracy in America*, ed. Phillips Bradley, trans. Henry Reeve (New York: Alfred A. Knopf, 1976).

16. Strickland, *How to Get into Law School*, 17.

17. Attributed to John Naisbitt, American writer. Quoted in Nash and Zullo, *Lawyer's Wit*, 167.

18. Fred Rodell, *Woe Unto You, Lawyers!* 2d ed. (New York: Pageant, 1957), 3.

19. For an excellent discussion of the history of the regulation of law and lawyers, see Anton-Herman Chroust, *The Rise of the Legal Profession in America*, 2 vols. (Norman: University of Oklahoma Press, 1965).

20. Stanley W. Lindberg, *The Annotated McGuffey* (New York: Van Nostrand Reinhold, 1976), 82.

21. The classic discussion of the *McGuffey Readers'* content is found in Richard D. Mosier, *Making the American Mind: Social and Moral Ideas in the McGuffey Readers* (New York: Columbia University, 1947). Also, see generally John H. Westerhoff, *McGuffey and His Readers: Piety, Morality, and Education in Nineteenth-Century America* (Nashville, TN: Abingdon, 1978).

22. Robert Karl Gilmore, *Ozark Baptizings, Hangings and Other Diversions* (Norman: University of Oklahoma Press, 1984), 200.

23. Ibid.

24. Edward Everett Dale, *Frontier Ways* (Austin: University of Texas Press, 1959), 182.

25. Lawrence W. Friedman, *Law in America: A Short History* (New York: Modern Library, 2002), 16.

26. Quoted in Nash and Zullo, *Lawyer's Wit*, 36.

27. Quoted in Tony Lyons, ed., *The Quotable Lawyer* (Guilford, CT: Lyons, 2002), 64.

28. Quoted in Nash and Zullo, *Lawyer's Wit*, 30.

29. Quoted ibid., 166.

30. Law and lawyer games, both board and video, are increasingly popular and controversial. These include Sue the Bastards! Sue Your Friends—Get Their Things, Justice: The Role Playing Game of the '20s and '30s, and Judge Dredd: The Game of Crime Fighting in Mega City One.

Chapter 2

1. American Bar Association, *National Lawyer Population by State,* http://www.abanet.org/marketresearch/2006_national%20_lawyer_population_survey.pdf.

2. See generally American Bar Association, *Lawyer Demographics,* http://www.abanet.org/marketresearch/lawyer_demographics_2006.pdf.

3. National Association of Law Placement, *Research and Directories,* http://www.nalp.org/research/index.php.

4. An interesting article discussing the legal profession in Japan is Gino Dal Pont, "The Social Status of the Legal Professions in Japan and the United States: A Structural and Cultural Analysis," *University of Detroit Mercy Law Review* 72 (Winter 1995): 291–326, available at http://members.cox.net/sbettwy/comparative6.Japan2.htm.

5. *The New Yorker Book of Lawyer Cartoons* (New York: Alfred A. Knopf, 2005), 3.

6. Marc Galanter, "The Day after the Litigation Explosion," *Maryland Law Review* 46 (Fall 1986): 3–39, as cited in Deborah Rhode and David Luban, eds., *Legal Ethics,* 4th ed. (New York: Foundation, 2004).

7. Rhode and Luban, *Legal Ethics,* 824.

8. The statistical information in this book is compiled from several sources and changes periodically to reflect revised and current data. For general information, see American Bar Association, *Market Research Department,* http://www.abanet.org/marketresearch/.

9. See "Federal Court Management Statistics," *U.S. Courts,* http://www.uscourts.gov/cgi-bin/cmsd2006.pl.

10. See generally, Eric Moller, *Trends in Civil Jury Verdicts since 1985* (Santa Monica, CA: Rand Institute for Social Justice, 1996). For this section, information was also gathered from multiple pages at *U.S. Courts,* http://www.uscourts.gov/.

11. Attributed to President Jimmy Carter in a speech given by Marilyn L. Pilkington in a presentation entitled "Challenges Facing the Legal Profession" at the Empire Club of Canada, at Toronto, Ontario, on April

27, 1995. Reprinted in John A. Campion and Edward P. Badinovac, eds., *The Empire Club of Canada Speeches, 1994–1995* (Toronto: Empire Club Foundation, 1995), 143–54. For a transcript of Pilkington's speech, see Empire Club Foundation, *Empire Club Addresses,* http://www.empireclubfoundation.com/details.asp?SpeechID=1273&FT=yes.

12. For example, a recent study of unmet needs in the state of Montana found that more than 80 percent of the population that did not have adequate legal assistance.

13. See generally Rennard Strickland and Gloria Valencia-Weber, "Observations on the Evolution of Indian Law in the Law Schools," *New Mexico Law Review* 26, no. 2 (1996): 153–68, and sources cited therein.

14. *MacPherson v. Buick Motor Co.,* 111 N.E. 1050 (1916). *MacPherson* is one of the cases featured in Foundation Press's series on famous cases by subject matter area. See James A. Henderson Jr., "*MacPherson v. Buick Motor Co.*: Simplifying the Facts While Reshaping the Law," in *Torts Stories,* ed. Robert A. Rabin and Stephen D. Sugarman (New York: Foundation, 2003), 41–71.

15. See generally Erik Erikson, *Childhood and Society* (New York: W. W. Norton, 1993).

16. Daniel J. Boorstin, *The Americans: The Democratic Experience* (New York: Random House, 1973), 53–64.

17. Catherine Crier, *The Case against Lawyers: How Lawyers, Politicians, and Bureaucrats Have Turned the Law into an Instrument of Tyranny—And What We as Citizens Have to Do about It* (New York: Broadway, 2003), 1.

18. Taunya Lovell Banks, "*To Kill a Mockingbird* (1962): Lawyering in an Unjust Society," as cited in *Screening Justice—The Cinema of Law: Significant Films of Law, Order and Social Justice,* ed. Rennard Strickland, Teree E. Foster, and Taunya Lovell Banks (Buffalo, NY: Hein, 2006), 239–52.

19. Darrow's perspective can be found in his autobiography, Clarence Darrow, *Story of My Life* (New York: Da Capo, 1996).

20. Will Durant and Ariel Durant, *The Lessons of History* (New York: Simon and Schuster, 1968).

21. Quoted in Tony Lyons, ed., *The Quotable Lawyer* (Guilford, CT: Lyons, 2002), 32.

22. Attributed to John J. Curtin Jr., American lawyer. Quoted in Bruce Nash and Allan Zullo, eds., *Lawyer's Wit and Wisdom: Quotations on the Legal Profession, in Brief* (Philadelphia: Running Press, 1995), 39.

23. See generally Rennard Strickland, *Fire and the Spirits* (Norman: University of Oklahoma Press, 1975).

24. Hillary Rodham Clinton, *It Takes a Village: And Other Lessons Children Teach Us* (New York: Simon and Schuster, 1996).

25. Quoted in Nash and Zullo, *Lawyer's Wit*, 62.

26. Quoted ibid., 58.

27. The official case citation is *Liebeck v. McDonald's Restaurants, P.T.S., Inc.,* 1995 WL 360309, N.M. Dist., 1994 (not reported in P.2d). There are many interesting articles about this case available on the Internet—and many that are quite egregiously opinionated in their presentation of the "facts" and of this case as a whole. For a factual account of this case, see Consumer Attorneys of California, *ATLA Fact Sheet,* http://caoc.com/CA/index.cfm?event=showPage&pg=facts.

28. Carl T. Bogus, *Why Lawsuits Are Good for America: Disciplined Democracy, Big Business, and the Common Law* (New York: New York University Press, 2001), 20–21.

29. Ibid., 29. See also Tom Baker, *The Medical Malpractice Myth* (Chicago: University of Chicago Press, 2005).

30. *Proctor v. Davis,* 682 N.E.2d 1203 (Ill. App. Ct. 1997); *Vandevender v. Sheetz, Inc.,* 490 S.E.2d 678 (W.Va. 1997).

31. For a complete discussion of the senator and the litigation, see Bogus, *Why Lawsuits Are Good for America,* 6–29. The Danforth speech is reproduced at page 7.

32. See generally the American Tort Reform Association Web site, http://www.atra.org (follow the "Looney Lawsuits" link). However, the "Pickled Justice" story is no longer listed on the Web site.

33. Laura Beth Nielsen and Aaron Beim, "Media Misrepresentation: Title VII, Print Media, and Public Perceptions of Discrimination Litigation," *Stanford Law and Policy Review* 15 (2004): 237–66. For a more detailed study of the distorted reporting of tort cases, see William Haltom and Michael McCann, *Distorting the Law: Politics, Media, and the Litigation Crisis* (Chicago: University of Chicago Press, 1998).

34. *Clifton v. Mass. Bay Transp. Auth.,* 11 Mass. L. Rep. 316 (Mass. Super. Ct. 2000)

35. For information on the AMA's views on malpractice verdicts, see the American Medical Association Web site, http://www.ama-assn.org.

36. Haltom and McCann, *Distorting the Law.*

37. See generally the National Association of Insurance Commissioners' Web site, http://www.naic.org.

38. Some sources have quoted that the actual losses were as high as $108 million. See generally, http://www.lasvegasweekly.com/2002/04_25/news_controversy_index.html.

39. This figure is very controversial. "Death by Medicine," according to Gerry Spence, "is now the leading killer and cause of injury in this

country, ahead of the prior champion killers, heart attacks and cancer." He further argues that "the latest composite figures show death by improper medical conduct of hospitals and doctors at 783,936 dead each year." Gerry Spence, *Bloodthirsty Bitches and Pious Pimps of Power* (New York: St. Martin's, 2006), 167. See also *Institute of Medicine,* http://www.iom.edu.

40. The NPDB has recently been renamed as the National Practitioner Data Bank and Healthcare Integrity and Protection Data Bank. For more information, see the group's Web site, http://www.npdb-hipdb.com.

41. Bob Herbert, "Medical Malpractice Lawsuits: Do We Have a Crisis or Insurance Industry Sham?" *New York Times,* June 25, 2004.

42. Laura Parker, "Medical-Malpractice Battle Gets Personal," *USA Today,* June 14, 2004.

43. Ibid.

44. For a detailed discussion of tort reform in Texas, see Terry Carter, "Tort Reform Texas Style," *ABA Journal* (October 2006): 30–36.

45. These statistics were set out in the *ABA Journal* (February 2007): 42, in an inset article entitled "Fighting with Footnotes." Available at http://www.abanet.org/journal/redesign/o2fatla.html. For a thoughtful discussion of data in the context of litigation, see D. Christopher Ohly, "DICTA: Lawyers on Trial—Litigators Become Scapegoats for America's Real Problems," *Virginia Law Weekly* 57, no. 8 (2004): 1, 6.

46. Jay Angoff, *Falling Claims and Rising Premiums in the Medical Malpractice Insurance Industry* (New York: Center for Justice and Democracy, 2005).

47. Bob Herbert, "Medical Malpractice Lawsuits."

48. Quoted in Nash and Zullo, *Lawyer's Wit,* 58.

49. Quoted in Elizabeth Frost-Knappman and David S. Shrager, eds., *A Concise Encyclopedia of Legal Quotations* (New York: Barnes and Noble Books, 2003), 214.

50. Calvin Woodard, "Reality and Social Reform: The Transition from Laissez-Faire to the Welfare State," *Yale Law Journal* 72, no. 2 (1962): 286–328.

51. Alexis de Tocqueville, *Democracy in America,* ed. Phillips Bradley, trans. Henry Reeve (New York: Alfred A. Knopf, 1976).

52. *Roe v. Wade,* 410 U.S. 113 (1973).

53. It is very difficult to arrive at an exact figure, which depends on whether an individual is a homeowner, renter, resident in a multifamily units, and so on. Estimates vary from three to seven years. For some general information about the effect of America's mobility, see Raymond Chretien, "Why Are Americans So Successful?" speech, Université de Montréal, Montréal, Québec, September 24, 2004, available at *Centre*

d'Études et de Recherches Internationales, http://www.cerium.ca/article154.html. The Employee Relocation Council in Washington, D.C., outlines the varied factors associated with moving. They conclude that about 40 million Americans move each year. Allison Stein Wellner, "Demographics: Amazing Facts about Moving," *USA Weekend,* May 11–13, 2007, 29.

54. There is a similar Russian proverb: "When God wanted to chastise mankind, He invented lawyers." Quoted in Nash and Zullo, *Lawyer's Wit,* 45.

55. Catherine Fennelly, *The Country Lawyer in New England, 1790–1840* (Sturbridge, MA: Old Sturbridge Village, 1968).

56. Robert E. Scott, "The Lawyer as Public Citizen," *University of Toledo Law Review* 31, no. 4 (2000).

Chapter 3

1. In each of the areas below, we have cited a general source to which one may turn for more information in that field. See generally Joy M. Feinman, *Law 101: Everything You Need to Know about the American Legal System,* 2d ed. (New York: Oxford University Press, 2006). A standard text for the nonlawyer is John J. Bonsignore, Ethan Katsh, Peter d'Errico, Ronald M. Pipken, and Stephen Arons, *Before the Law: An Introduction to the Legal Process* (Atlanta: Houghton Mifflin, 1974).

2. George T. Bogert, *Bogert's Hornbook on Trusts,* 6th ed. (St. Paul, MN: West Law School, 1987); Thomas E. Atkinson, *Atkinson's Hornbook on Wills,* 2d ed. (St. Paul, MN: West Law School, 1953); American Bar Association, *The American Bar Association Guide to Wills and Estates,* 2d ed. (New York: Random House Information Group, 2004).

3. John D. Calamari and Joseph M. Perillo, *Calamari and Perillo's Handbook on Contracts,* 5th ed. (St. Paul, MN: West Law School, 2003); Arthur L. Corbin, *Corbin's Text on Contracts,* student ed. (St. Paul, MN: West Law School, 1952).

4. Dan B. Dobbs, *Dobbs' Hornbook on the Law of Torts* (St. Paul, MN: West Law School, 2000); Dan B. Dobbs, Robert E. Keeton, W. Page Keeton, David G. Owen, and William L. Prosser, *Prosser and Keeton's Hornbook on Torts,* 5th ed. (St. Paul, MN: West Law School, 1984).

5. Wayne R. LaFave, *LaFave's Hornbook on Criminal Law,* 4th ed. (St. Paul, MN: West Law School, 2003).

6. Charles A. Shanor and L. Lynn Hogue, *Shanor and Hogue's National Security and Military Law in a Nutshell* (St. Paul, MN: West Law School, 2003); Jonathan Turley, "What Our Soldiers Really Need: Lawyers," *USA Today,* April 12, 2007.

7. Alfred C. Aman Jr. and William T. Mayton, *Aman and Mayton's Hornbook on Administrative Law,* 2d ed. (St. Paul, MN: West Law School, 2001).

8. Homer H. Clark, *Clark's Hornbook on the Law of Domestic Relations in the United States,* 2d ed. (St. Paul, MN: West Law School, 1998); American Bar Association, *The American Bar Association Guide to Marriage, Divorce and Families* (New York: Random House Information Group, 2006).

9. All of these rights are enumerated in the U.S. Constitution and its amendments, and they have been clarified by judicial cases which have implemented further protections, such as the recitation of Miranda rights upon arrest, what constitutes questioning by the police, how to select a fair and impartial jury, and so on. There are literally hundreds, if not thousands of books on the market today that review the rights of citizens guaranteed by the Constitution and explain how they apply to our everyday lives. Every citizen should take the time to learn about the rights that they have under these foundational principles. For more information, the authors recommend a series of books authored by the American Civil Liberties Union (ACLU).

10. 15 U.S.C. §§ 1–2. For a discussion about the Sherman Act from the U.S. government, see Federal Trade Commission, *An Antitrust Primer,* http://www.ftc.gov/bc/compguide/antitrst.htm.

11. *U.S. v. American Tobacco Co.,* 221 U.S. 106 (1911).

12. 15 U.S.C. §§ 78d-3, 780-6, 7201, 7202, 7211–19, 7231–34, 7241–46, 7261–66 (2002), and 18 U.S.C. §§ 1348–50, 1514A, 1519, 1520 (2002).

13. Leviticus 24:22 (AV) (sometimes referred to as the "an eye for an eye" passage).

14. Daniel Webster, as found at The Other Pages, *Quotations Home Page,* http://www.theotherpages.org/topic-j2.html.

Chapter 4

1. On a recent Internet search for information about this case, of the first one hundred entries mentioning this case, only two included information about the dismissal of the case. One such article is Associated Press, *McDonald's Wins Fat Fight,* CBS News, January 22, 2003, available at *CBS News.com,* http://www.cbsnews.com/stories/2003/01/22/health/main537520.shtml.

2. For the governor's response, see *State of Wisconsin, Office of the Governor,* "Veto Message," http://www.wisgov.state.wi.us/docs/031704VetoMessage _AB595.pdf.

3. The twelve states were Arizona, Colorado, Florida, Georgia, Idaho, Illinois, Louisiana, Missouri, South Dakota, Tennessee, Utah, and Washington. See generally *Stateline,* http://www.stateline.org.

4. A dismissal may be had for a variety of causes: (1) lack of jurisdiction over the subject matter, (2) lack of jurisdiction over the person, (3) improper venue, (4) insufficiency of process, (5) insufficiency of service of process, (6) failure to state a claim upon which relief can be granted, or (7) failure to join a party. See Rule 12(b) of the Federal Rules of Civil Procedure (Fed. R. Civ. P.).

5. Rule 12(c), Fed. R. Civ. P.

6. Rule 56, Fed. R. Civ. P.

7. Rule 50, Fed. R. Civ. P.

8. Rule 11, Fed. R. Civ. P.

9. See Rule 3.1 of the Model Rules of Professional Conduct (M.R.P.C.) promulgated by the American Bar Association and adopted in some form by most state bar associations.

10. *Daubert v. Merrell Dow Pharmaceuticals, Inc.*, 509 U.S. 579 (1993).

11. For the American Bar Association's explanation of contingent fees, see American Bar Association, *Legal Fees and Expenses*, http://www.abanet .org/publiced/practical/lawyerfees_contingent.html.

12. For general provisions regarding an award of costs and attorney fees, see Rule 54(d), Fed. R. Civ. P. For examples of statutes that specifically provide for the award of attorney fees, see 42 U.S.C. § 1988 (proceedings in vindication of civil rights) and 17 U.S.C. § 505 (copyright infringement and remedies).

13. Punitive damages: "Damages awarded in addition to actual damages when the defendant acted with recklessness, malice, or deceit; specifically, damages assessed by way of penalizing the wrongdoer or making an example to others." *Black's Law Dictionary*, 8th ed. (St. Paul, MN: West, 1999), 418.

14. See generally U.S. Department of Justice, *Rights of the People*, "Rights of the Accused," http://usinfo.state.gov/products/pubs/rightsof/accused.htm.

15. Robert MacCrate, ed., *Legal Education and Professional Development—An Educational Continuum*, student ed. (St. Paul, MN: West, 1992). General information on minority and other programs are available from the Law School Admission Council in Newtown, PA, or by visiting the organization's Web site, http://www.lsac.org.

16. See generally American Bar Association, *Continuing Legal Education*, http://www.abanet.org/cle/home.html.

17. See the University of Oregon School of Law Web site, http://www .law.uoregon.edu/org/probono/docs/newsletter.pdf.

18. Dennis W. Archer, "President's Message—Three for All: A Trio of Entities Support ABA Efforts to Address Pressing Issues of the Day," *ABA Journal* (March 2004): 8.

19. Again, there is much information available on this topic for anyone interested in additional information. A recent search of the Web for "legal reform" returned almost 1.25 million Web hits.

Chapter 5

1. *Brown v. Board of Ed. of Topeka,* Shawnee County, Kan., 347 U.S. 483 (1954).

2. Frank T. Read and Lucy S. McGough, *Let Them Be Judged: The Judicial Integration of the Deep South* (Metuchen, NJ: Scarecrow, 1978).

3. *Brown v. Board of Ed. of Topeka, Kan.,* 349 U.S. 294 (1955).

4. Read and McGough, *Let Them Be Judged,* 111.

5. *Parents Involved in Community Schools v. Seattle School District No. 1,* No. 05-908 (argued Dec. 4, 2006, decided June 28, 2007). Decided together with *Meredith, Custodial Parent and Next Friend of McDonald v. Jefferson County Bd. of Ed.,* No. 05-915.

6. *United States v. Washington,* 520 F.2d 676 (9th Cir. 1975). A touching human presentation of the fishing rights struggle is found in Charles Wilkinson, *Messages from Frank's Landing* (Seattle: University of Washington Press, 2000).

7. Rennard Strickland, Stephen J. Herzberg, and Steven R. Owens, *Keeping Our Word: Indian Treaty Rights and Public Responsibilities. A Report on a Recommended Federal Role Following Wisconsin's Request for Federal Assistance. Prepared for the Senate Select Committee on Indian Affairs* (unpublished report, Madison, University of Wisconsin, 1990).

8. To review the Master Settlement Agreement, see the Web site of the National Association of Attorneys General, http://www.naag.org/tobac/cigmsa.rtf.

9. See PBS, *Frontline,* "Inside the Tobacco Deal," http://www.pbs.org/wgbh/pages/frontline/shows/settlement.

10. See http://pqasb.pqarchiver.com/latimes/access.

11. U.S. Const. Am. V; *Kelo v. City of New London, Conn.,* 545 U.S. 469 (2005).

12. *United States ex rel. Caminito v. Murphy,* 222 F.2d 698, 706 (2d Cir. 1955).

13. See generally the Interest on Lawyers Trust Accounts Web site, http://iolta.org.

14. See generally American Bar Association, *Rule of Law Initiative,* "Europe and Eurasia," http://www.abanet.org/rol/europe_and_eurasia/.

15. Robert A. Stein, "Executive Director's Report—Reaching Our Goals: The Standing Committee on Legal Aid and Indigent Defendants Leads the Way," *ABA Journal* (June 2004): 65.

16. Deborah L. Rhode, *In the Interests of Justice: Refining the Legal Profession* (New York: Oxford University Press, 2000).

17. Ibid., 208, 213.

18. William Hogarth, "Credulity, Superstition and Fanaticism" (1762) as reproduced in Sean Shesgreen, ed., *Engravings by Hogarth* (New York: Dover, 1973), plate 95.

19. See generally *Science Encyclopedia, The History of Ideas,* vol. 3, "Generation," http://science.jrank.org/pages/7721/Generation.html.

20. For a more detailed discussion of the many problems associated with this case, see Stuart Taylor Jr. and K. C. Johnson, *Until Proven Innocent: Political Correctness and the Shameful Injustice of the Duke Lacrosse Rape Case* (New York: St. Martin's, 2007); and Don Yaeger and Mike Pressler, *It's Not about the Truth: The Untold Story of the Duke Lacrosse Case and the Lives It Shattered* (New York: Threshold Editions, 2007).

21. Other Texas chief justices have also fought for change, both while in office and afterward. Chief Justice Robert W. Calvert (1961–72) chaired the Constitutional Revision Commission of 1973. Its proposal, which placed merit election in a new Texas Constitution, was not adopted. Chief Justice John L. Hill (1985–88) resigned midway through his first term to fight for selection reform. As a former attorney general and gubernatorial candidate, he continues to be the state's leading voice for choosing judges based on merit.

22. While he is often credited with having said this, verification of the quote has been elusive. For more information about Justice Hugo Black, see generally *Hugo Black of Alabama,* http://www.hugoblack.com, and "Black, Hugo Lafayette," *Biographical Directory of the United States Congress,* http://bioguide.congress.gov/scripts/biodisplay.pl?index=B000499.

23. Alexis de Tocqueville, *Democracy in America,* ed. Phillips Bradley, trans. Henry Reeve (New York: Alfred A. Knopf, 1976).

Chapter 6

1. Prospective law students are referred to Wendy Margolis, Bonnie Gordon, and David Rosenlieb, eds., *ABA LSAC Official Guide to ABA-Approved Law Schools,* 2008 ed. (Newtown, PA: Law School Admission Council, 2007).

2. Rennard Strickland, *How to Get into Law School* (New York: Hawthorn Books, 1974), 17. For examples of the lives of a group of lawyers who lived greatly, see Norman Gross, ed., *Noble Purposes: Nine Champions of the Rule of Law* (Athens: Ohio University Press, 2007). See also Peter Irons, *The Courage of Their Convictions: Sixteen Americans Who Fought Their Way to the Supreme Court* (New York: Free Press, 1988); "Symposium: When a Lawyer Stood

Tall: Sharing and Understanding Stories of Lawyer Heroes," *Widener Law Journal* 13, no. 1 (2003); Frederick S. Voss, *Portraits of the American Law* (Washington, DC: National Portrait Gallery of the Smithsonian Institution, 1989); George S. Grossman, ed., *The Spirit of American Law* (Boulder, CO: Westview, 2000).

3. Victor Cook to Rennard Strickland, Rennard Strickland Collection, archives Northeastern State University, Tahlequah, OK.

4. Joan Hill to Rennard Strickland, Rennard Strickland Collection.

5. T. S. Eliot, *The Confidential Clerk* (New York: Harcourt, 1950).

6. Andy Watson, lecture, University of Virginia School of Law, September 1962.

7. Thomas Wolfe, *Look Homeward, Angel* (New York: Scribner's, 1929).

8. Herbert Wechsler, *Harlan Fiske Stone*, http://www.supremecourthistory .org/04_library/subs_volumes/04_c10_l.html.

9. Quoted in dean's message, Carolyn Jones, University of Iowa College of Law. See University of Iowa College of Law, *A Message from the Dean*, 2007, http://www.law.uiowa.edu/dean/index.php.

10. This quote is often attributed to Dante Alighieri, sometimes as part of *The Divine Comedy;* however, it has also sometimes been attributed to Thomas Aquinas.

11. Frank T. Read, *Recollections of South Texas*, statement March 2007. In a broader context, for a discussion of integrity in law, see Stephen L. Carter, *Integrity* (New York: Basic Books, 1996).

12. Strickland, *How to Get into Law School*, viii.

13. Crazy Horse, September 23, 1875. See generally http://www .nativeamericans.com/ and http://www.lakotawritings.com/Quotes.html.

14. Oliver Wendell Holmes Jr., quoted in Clifton Fadiman, ed., *The Little, Brown Book of Anecdotes* (Boston: Little, Brown, 1985), 285.

15. Quoted in Strickland, *How to Get into Law School*, 146.

FURTHER READING

Arron, Deborah L. *Running from the Law: Why Good Lawyers Are Getting out of the Legal Profession*. Seattle, WA: Niche, 1989.

Auerbach, Jerold S. *Justice without Law? Resolving Disputes without Lawyers*. New York: Oxford University Press, 1983.

Bachman, Walt. *Law v. Life: What Lawyers Are Afraid to Say about the Legal Profession*. Rhinebeck, NY: Four Directions, 1995.

Bell, Peter A., and Jeffrey O'Connell. *Accidental Justice: The Dilemma of Tort Law*. New Haven, CT: Yale University Press, 1997.

Bloomfield, Maxwell. *American Lawyers in a Changing Society, 1776–1876*. Cambridge, MA: Harvard University Press, 1976.

Brallier, Jess M., ed., *Lawyers and Other Reptiles*. Chicago: Contemporary Books, 1992.

Brodeur, Paul. *Outrageous Misconduct: The Asbestos Industry on Trial*. New York: Pantheon, 1985.

Burke, Thomas F. *Lawyers, Lawsuits and Legal Rights: The Battle over Litigation in American Society*. Berkeley: University of California Press, 2002.

Crier, Catherine. *The Case against Lawyers: How Lawyers, Politicians and Bureaucrats Have Turned the Law into an Instrument of Tyranny—And What We as Citizens Have to Do about It*. New York: Broadway, 2002.

Fleming, Macklin. *Lawyers, Money and Success*. Westport, CT: Quorum, 1997.

Fletcher, George P. *With Justice for Some*. Reading, PA: Addison-Wesley, 1995.

Frank, Jerome. *Courts on Trial*. Princeton, NJ: Princeton University Press, 1949.

Frankel, Marvin E. *Partisan Justice*. New York: Hill and Wang, 1980.

Friedman, Lawrence W. *Total Justice*. New York: Russell Sage Foundation, 1994.

Galanter, Marc, and Thomas Palay. *Tournament of Lawyers: The Transformation of the Big Law Firms*. Chicago: University of Chicago Press, 1991.

Garralt, Gerald, ed. *The New High Priests: Lawyers in Post–Civil War America*. Westport, CT: Greenwood, 1984.

Glendon, Mary Ann. *A Nation under Lawyers*. New York: Farrar, Straus and Giroux, 1994.

Goulden, Joseph C. *The Superlawyers: The Small and Powerful World of the Great Washington Law Firms*. New York: Weybright and Talley, 1972.

Grace, Nancy, and Diane Clehane. *Objection! How High-Priced Defense Attorneys, Celebrity Defendants, and a 24/7 Media Have Hijacked Our Criminal Justice System*. New York: Hyperion, 2005.

Gross, Norman, ed. *America's Lawyer-Presidents: From Law Office to Oval Office*. Evanston, IL: Northwestern University Press, 2004.

Guinier, Lani, Michelle Fine, and Jane Balin. *Becoming Gentlemen: Women, Law School and Institutional Change*. Cambridge, MA: Harvard University Press, 1997.

Howard, Philip K. *The Death of Common Sense: How Law Is Suffocating America*. New York: Warner, 1994.

Joseph, Lawrence. *Lawyerland: What Lawyers Talk about When They Talk about Law*. New York: Farrar, Straus and Giroux, 1997.

Kronman, Anthony T. *The Lost Lawyer: Failing Ideals of the Legal Profession*. Cambridge, MA: Harvard University Press, 1993.

Linowitz, Sol M., and Martin Mayer. *The Betrayed Profession*. New York: Charles Scribner's Sons, 1994.

Litan, Robert E. *Verdict: Assessing the Civil Jury System*. New York: Norton, 1991.

Nader, Ralph, and Wesley Smith. *No Contest: Corporate Lawyers and the Perversion of Justice in America*. New York: Random House, 1996.

Nelson, Robert L. *Partners with Power: Social Transformation of the Large Law Firm*. Berkeley: University of California Press, 1988.

Nelson, Robert L., David M. Trubek, and Raymond L. Solomon. *Lawyers' Ideals/Lawyers' Practices*. Ithaca, NY: Cornell University Press, 1992.

Olson, Walter K. *The Excuse Factory: How Employment Law Is Paralyzing America*. New York: Free Press, 1997.

———. *The Litigator Explosion: What Happened When America Unleashed the Lawsuit*. New York: Penguin, 1991.

———. *The Rule of Lawyers: How the New Litigation Elite Threatens America's Rule of Law*. New York: St. Martin's Griffin, 2004.

O'Reilly, Bill. *Who's Looking Out for You?* New York: Broadway, 2003.

Perry, Susan, and Jim Dawson. *Nightmare: Women and the Dalkon Shield*. New York: Macmillan, 1985.

Pizzi, William T. *Trials without Truth*. New York: New York University Press, 1997.

Pringle, Peter. *Cornered: Big Tobacco at the Bar of Justice*. New York: Henry Holt, 1998.

Rhode, Deborah L. *In the Interest of Justice: Reforming the Legal Profession*. Oxford: Oxford University Press, 2001.

Robinson, Mathew B. *Justice Blind?* Englewood Cliffs, NJ: Prentice Hall, 2002.

Rodell, Fred. *Woe Unto You Lawyers!* 2d ed. New York: Pageant, 1957.

Rose, Derek. "Robertson: Judges Worse Than Al Qaeda." *New York Daily News*, May 2, 2005.

Rosenberg, Gerald N. *The Hollow Hope: Can the Courts Bring about Social Change?* Chicago: University of Chicago Press, 1991.

Ross, William G. *The Hardest Hour: The Ethics of Time-Based Billing by Attorneys*. Durham, NC: Carolina Academic Press, 1996.

Rothwax, Harold J. *Guilty: The Collapse of Criminal Justice*. New York: Random House, 1996.

Schaffer, Thomas L., and Mary M. Schaffer. *American Lawyers and Their Communities*. Notre Dame, IN: University of Notre Dame Press, 1991.

Schlag, Pierre. *Laying Down the Law*. New York: New York University Press, 1996.

Schuck, Peter H., ed. *Tort Law and the Public Interest: Competitor Innovation and Consumer Welfare*. New York: Norton, 1991.

Spence, Gerry. *Bloodthirsty Bitches and Pious Pimps of Power*. New York: St. Martin's, 2006.

Stenart, James B. *The Partners*. New York: Simon and Schuster, 1983.

Stevens, Mark. *The Power of Attorney: The Rise of the Giant Law Firms*. New York: McGraw-Hill, 1987.

Stossel, John. *Give Me a Break: How I Exposed Hucksters, Cheats, and Scam Artists and Became the Scourge of the Liberal Media*. New York: HarperCollins, 2004.

———. *Myths, Lies and Downright Stupidity*. New York: Hyperion, 2006.

Strickland, Rennard. "Continuity and Change in Legal Education," *University of Tulsa Law Journal* 10, no. 2 (1974): 225–30.

———. "A Demon-Crossed Generation That Said Yes," *University of Tulsa Law Journal* 11, no. 1 (1975): 54–57

———. "The Lawyer as Modern Medicine Man." *Southern Illinois University Law Journal* 11, no. 1 (1986): 203–16.

———. "The Lawyer as Secular Priest: A Call for Attorneys Who Are More Than Legal Engineers." *Learning and the Law* 3, no. 3 (1976): 40–43.

Trotter, Michael. *Profit and the Practice of Law.* Athens: University of Georgia Press 1997.

Van Susteren, Greta, and Elaine Lafferty. *My Turn at the Bully Pulpit: Straight Talk about the Things That Drive Me Nuts.* New York: Crown, 2003.

Zitrin, Richard, and Carol M. Langsford. *The Moral Compass of the American Lawyer.* New York: Ballantine, 1999.

Further Reading

ABOUT THE AUTHORS

Rennard Strickland and Frank T. Read are two of America's most experienced legal educators. In almost three-quarters of a century in higher education, they have held nine deanships, taught at more than twenty-five law schools, published more than forty books, and helped prepare thousands of students to become lawyers.

Strickland, a graduate of the University of Virginia School of Law, is Phillip H. Knight Professor of Law emeritus at the University of Oregon, where he served as dean from 1997 to 2002. He also served as dean at three additional law schools and taught at more than a dozen others. Strickland is the only person ever to have served both as president of the Association of American Law Schools and as chair of the Law School Admissions Council. Strickland has been honored by the American Bar Association with its Spirit of Excellence Award and by the Society of American Law Teachers with the annual SALT Award for contribution to legal education and the cause of legal reform. His academic and teaching fields include Native American law, legal history, the legal profession, legal anthropology, and law in popular culture. Strickland was the founding director of the Center for the Study of American Indian Law and Policy at the University of Oklahoma, where he currently is a scholar in residence.

His published works include *Tonto's Revenge, The Handbook of Federal Indian Law* (editor), *How to Get into Law School, Fire and the Spirits,* and *The Prelaw Handbook* (editor).

Read, a graduate of the Duke University School of Law, is former president and dean of South Texas College of Law, where he is currently a law professor. Read has served as dean at five law schools, including the University of California/Hastings College of the Law, the University of Florida, Indiana University–Indianapolis, and the University of Tulsa. Read served as president of the Law School Admissions Council, as chairman of the Board of Law Access, Inc., and as deputy consultant to the American Bar Association Section on Legal Education and Admission to the Bar. He has been honored for his contributions to education in lawyering skills. His academic and teaching fields include evidence, trial practice, ethics and professional responsibility, civil procedure, and torts. Among his published works are *Let Them Be Judged: The Judicial Integration of the Deep South, Oklahoma Evidence Handbook,* and *Read's Florida Evidence.*